D1224596

Essential Histories

The Falklands War 1982

Essential Histories

The Falklands War 1982

Duncan Anderson

First published in Great Britain in 2002 by Osprey Publishing,
Elms Court, Chapel Way, Botley, Oxford OX2 9LP
Email: info@ospreypublishing.com

© 2002 Osprey Publishing Ltd.

All rights reserved. Apart from any fair dealing for the purpose
of private study, research, criticism or review, as permitted under
the Copyright, Designs and Patents Act, 1988, no part of this
publication may be reproduced, stored in a retrieval system, or
transmitted in any form or by any means, electronic, electrical,
chemical, mechanical, optical, photocopying, recording or
otherwise, without the prior written permission of the copyright
owner. Enquiries should be addressed to the Publishers.

Every attempt has been made by the Publishers to secure the
appropriate permissions for material reproduced in this book. If
there has been any oversight we will be happy to rectify the
situation and written submissions should be made to the
Publishers.

ISBN 1 84176 422 1

Editor: Rebecca Cullen
Design: Ken Vail Graphic Design, Cambridge, UK
Cartography by The Map Studio
Index by Alan Thatcher
Picture research by Image Select International
Origination by Grasmere Digital Imaging, Leeds, UK
Printed and bound in China by L. Rex Printing Company Ltd.

02 03 04 05 06   10 9 8 7 6 5 4 3 2 1

For a complete list of titles available from Osprey Publishing
please contact:

Osprey Direct UK, PO Box 140,
Wellingborough, Northants, NN8 4ZA, UK.
Email: info@ospreydirect.co.uk

Osprey Direct USA,
c/o Motorbooks International, PO Box 1,
Osceola, WI 54020-0001, USA.
Email: info@ospreydirectusa.com

www.ospreypublishing.com

Contents

Introduction

In the spring of 1982 the largest task force Britain had assembled for a generation set sail to recapture the Falkland Islands from Argentina. It was one of the most desperate operations of war ever undertaken. The task force would be operating only 800 miles from the Antarctic continent, nearly 8,000 miles from its home base, with the onset of the South Atlantic winter only weeks away. The British knew that the Argentine air force would outnumber them more than 4 to 1, and that its pilots were amongst the most daring and skilful in the world. The Royal Navy were relying on missile systems that had never been tested in war to redress the balance. Many officers felt privately that aerial parity, let alone superiority, could not be achieved. The admiral commanding the task force knew that if the Argentines hit his carriers, or any of his large logistic vessels, the expedition would end in failure, and that this would deal a psychological blow to Britain from which she might not recover – at least not for many years. There was a sense that this conflict was not about the invasion of the Falklands per se, but about what that invasion represented. In its long history Britain had often gone to war when narrowly defined self-interest indicated that there was no need to do so. 1914 had been one such occasion, and 1939 another. So, too, was 1982.

Chronology

18–19 March Argentine scrap-metal workers land at Leith Harbour, South Georgia, and raise the Argentine flag: action reported by members of the British Antarctic Survey team.

21 March HMS *Endurance*, with small Royal Marine contingent aboard, leaves Port Stanley with instructions to arrange for departure of Argentines from South Georgia.

25 March Argentine Marines lands at Leith. Argentine naval units begin to leave home ports. British cabinet discusses crisis.

26 March Argentine Junta issues orders for dispatch of invasion force.

29 March Argentine Junta approves final plans for invasion of Falklands.

30 March Royal Marine reinforcements arrive at Port Stanley, bringing the garrison to a strength of 76 officers and men. British government decides to send naval units to South Atlantic.

31 March *Endurance* lands Royal Marine party on South Georgia. British commence preparations for establishment of task force for use in South Atlantic.

2 April Operation Rosario. Argentine troops invade Falklands. Having inflicted casualties on attackers, British forces are surrendered by Governor Rex Hunt. British cabinet agrees to order despatch of task force. In Plymouth first 'Orders' group of commanders takes place.

3 April Argentine Marines land at Grytviken, South Georgia, capturing Royal Marine defenders after brief firefight. UN Security Council adopts Resolution 502 (vote 10–1, four abstentions), which demands immediate cessation of hostilities and withdrawal of all Argentine forces from the Falklands, and which calls for a diplomatic solution to the crisis. Margaret Thatcher announces despatch of task force to recapture the islands.

5 April Lord Carrington resigns and is replaced as Foreign Secretary by Francis Pym. First elements of the task force (among them carriers *Invincible* and *Hermes*) sail from Portsmouth. Requisitioning of merchant vessels commences.

6 April Argentina commences reinforcement of forces in Falklands.

7 April Argentina creates South Atlantic Operational Theatre HQ. Britain declares maritime exclusion zone centred on Falklands and with 200 nautical mile radius, to come into effect 0400 hours 12 April. President Reagan approves Alexander Haig's peace mission. *Canberra* arrives at Southampton to undergo military conversions and to embark 3 Para and 40 and 42 Commandos. French government withdraws technical assistance teams from Argentina.

8 April *Canberra* sails from Southampton. Haig arrives in UK. UN Secretary General Perez de Cuellar establishes working group to develop plans in case of failure of US mediation. Further task force elements sail from Gibraltar.

9 April Haig arrives in Buenos Aires

10 April Discussions between Haig and Argentine representatives. First elements of naval task force arrive at Ascension Island.

12 April Maritime exclusion zone comes into effect. Haig returns to London for talks.

13 April Haig travels to Washington for debriefing.

14 April HMS *Intrepid* put back into commission. Container ship *Atlantic Conveyor* taken up from trade.

15 April Detailed planning for recapture of South Georgia and Falklands (Operation Corporate) commences. Haig flies to Buenos Aires.

17 April 'War Council' aboard HMS *Hermes*. Elements of the task force depart from Ascension Island. Argentine navy units, among them the carrier *Veinticinco de Mayo* and cruiser *General Belgrano* leave home ports. Haig meets Junta for talks.

18 April Further substantial task force elements depart Ascension.

21 April Argentine reconnaissance aircraft penetrates to within 12 miles of task force before retreating. HMS *Antrim* uses Wessex helicopter to land special forces on South Georgia.

22 April Special Forces evacuated from South Georgia due to poor weather conditions. Galtieri visits Port Stanley and decides to increase the size and speed of the build up.

25 April British helicopters engage Argentine submarine *Sante Fe* and drive it ashore on South Georgia in a damaged condition. Royal Marines and Special Forces (75 men) land on South Georgia (culmination of Operation Paraquat). Argentines surrender.

27 April Argentine navy deploys to counter anticipated British landing on Falklands.

28 April British government announces further restrictions on transit through 200 nautical mile exclusion zone (amounting to complete blockade), to come into effect 1100 hours 30 April. Further task force elements (requisitioned merchant vessels) concentrate at Ascension.

29 April Argentine fleet splits into two groups, one moving north-west, and the other south of the Falklands.

30 April Total exclusion zone comes into effect around Falklands. President Reagan announces support for Britain, offering military supplies and implementing sanctions against Argentina.

1 May Haig's peace mission fails. Pre-dawn raid by single Vulcan bomber on Port Stanley airfield (Op. Black Buck 1) followed up by Sea Harrier attacks and bombardments by naval task force; airfield remains open, Argentines lose four aircraft in abortive attacks on task force. British special forces land on East and West Falkland to recce possible landing sites. RMS *QE2* requisitioned.

2 May Peru offers new peace plan for solving crisis. UN offers similar services. However, at 1600 hrs HMS *Conqueror* sinks *General Belgrano* approx 35 miles south-west of exclusion zone. 323 Argentines perish.

3 May Argentine patrol vessel *Alferez Sobral* damaged by HMS *Coventry's* Lynx helicopter 90 miles inside exclusion zone. Admiral Anaya orders Argentine warships back to port.

4 May HMS *Sheffield* hit by air-launched Exocet missile south-east of Falklands. 20 crew killed, vessel abandoned. Operation Black Buck 2 Vulcan raid fails to inflict significant damage on Port Stanley airfield. One Sea Harrier shot down over Goose Green airfield.

5 May British Cabinet meets to discuss Peruvian initiative. Argentina formally accepts UN mediation.

6 May Britain formally accepts offer of UN mediation. Two Sea Harriers lost, probably to mid-air collision.

7 May Exclusion zone extended to within 12 miles of Argentina's coastline. UN Secretary General announces peace initiative. Main body of British amphibious forces leaves Ascension.

9 May Argentine intelligence vessel *Narwhal* (camouflaged as fishing trawler) attacked and boarded by British; Argentine helicopter shot down over Port Stanley.

10 May *Sheffield* sinks under tow. Argentine transport *Isla de los Estados* sunk by HMS *Alacrity* between East and West Falklands.

11 May British Nimrods commence operations in long-range reconnaissance role.

12 May Argentine Air Force launches major air effort against naval task force, inflicting slight damage but losing three Skyhawks. Decision made to land troops at San Carlos. *QE2* sails from Southampton with 5 Infantry Brigade aboard.

15 May In raid on Argentine airfield on Pebble Island, 45 members of SAS destroy ammunition dump and 11 aircraft.

19 May After a temporary lull in operations, preparations for landing commence following official Cabinet approval for operation. Sea King helicopter with SAS personnel aboard crashes.

20 May Sea King helicopter involved in special operation carries out forced landing in Chile; crew repatriated. After lengthy negotiations UN peace initiative breaks down. Second Peruvian peace plan announced.

21 May 4,000 troops of 2 Para, 3 Para, 40, 42 and 45 Royal Marine Commandos (with support services) land almost unopposed at San Carlos. Heavy air attacks on naval task force cost Argentines 11 aircraft (five Mirage, five Skyhawk, one Pucara), but latter succeed in sinking *Ardent*. Other vessels damaged. British lose one Harrier and two helicopters.

22 May Lull in air attacks allows substantial reinforcement of San Carlos bridgehead.

23 May In renewed air assault Argentines lose at least six more aircraft (as well as four helicopters elsewhere), but hit frigate *Antelope*. Attempt to defuse unexploded bombs aboard latter fails when one bomb explodes, and *Antelope* later sinks. Junta appoints General Garcia to run new Joint Operations Centre (CEOPECON) at Commodoro Rivadavia.

24 May Further air attacks; several Argentine aircraft shot down, light damage inflicted on British logistics landing ships.

25 May HMS *Coventry* and container vessel *Atlantic Conveyor* sunk, former by bombs and latter by air-launched Exocet. Three

Argentine aircraft destroyed. Air force commander Lami Dozo sends peace envoy to New York.

26 May UN adopts Resolution 505. Northwood demands that 3 Commando Brigade commence offensive operations. 2 Para advances towards Goose Green.

27 May 45 Commando and 3 Para leave bridgehead for Port Stanley. SAS airlifted forward. Successful Argentine air raids on logistics base at Ajax Bay. Vessels carrying 5 Brigade rendezvous near South Georgia.

28 May 2 Para (600 strong) commences attack on Darwin and Goose Green at 0230 hrs. After day-long battle with more numerous Argentine forces, objectives are captured. Approximately 1,300 prisoners are taken. Lieutenant Colonel 'H' Jones killed.

29 May 3 Para reaches Teal Inlet. 45 Commando sets off for Douglas.

30 May Further Argentine air attacks; two Skyhawks shot down, Major General Moore arrives in Falklands to command land forces. 45 Commando and 3 Para secure Douglas and Teal respectively on north side of East Falklands.

31 May Elements of 42 Commando and SAS airlifted to within 10 miles of Port Stanley (Mt Kent and Mt Challenger). Mountain and Arctic Warfare Cadre attack Argentine special forces at Top Malo House. 45 Commando reaches Teal Inlet. UN Secretary General proposes new peace plan.

1 June 5 Brigade commences disembarkation at San Carlos. 3 Commando Brigade forward base established at Teal Inlet. Aggressive patrolling carried out by 42 and 45 Commandos, and by 3 Para in direction of Port Stanley.

2 June Surrender leaflets dropped on Port Stanley. 2 Para elements airlifted to Bluff Cove.

3 June Versailles Summit opens. President Reagan presents five-point plan to British.

5 June Scots Guards embark on *Sir Tristram* for transport to Fitzroy–Bluff Cove area. Harrier airbase established at San Carlos.

6 June Scots Guards land at Fitzroy, establishing 5 Brigade forward base. Landings at San Carlos completed. British have around 8,000 troops on East Falkland.

7 June UN Secretary General announces another peace plan.

8 June *Sir Galahad* and *Sir Tristram* attacked by Argentine aircraft at Bluff Cove. *Sir Galahad* crippled, 46 killed and 150 injured (mainly Welsh Guards). Frigate HMS *Plymouth* damaged by air attack; several Argentine aircraft destroyed. Plan of attack on Port Stanley finalised.

11 June Supported by 105mm guns and a bombardment by the naval task force, 42 Commando attacks Mt Harriet and Goat Ridge; 45 Commando attacks Two Sisters; 3 Para attacks Mt Longdon (five miles west of Port Stanley). All objectives captured by the following morning.

12 June HMS *Glamorgan* damaged by Exocet fired from improvised land-based mounting.

13–14 June Second phase of attack on Port Stanley. 2 Para attack Wireless Ridge; Scots Guards attack Tumbledown; 1/7 Gurkhas occupy Mt William.

14 June After negotiations, Brigadier General Mario Menendez surrenders all Argentine forces in East and West Falkland. 11,400 prisoners are taken and subsequently repatriated.

21 June Port Stanley airfield opened for operations. *Sir Galahad* towed out to sea and sunk as a war grave.

12 July Britain announces that active hostilities over the Falklands are regarded as having ended; the Argentines fail to make any similar statement.

22 July Total exclusion zone lifted.

Tango and tea dance: Argentine and British misperceptions

In 1807 a British expeditionary force landed on the shores of the river Platte and marched on the Spanish colony of Buenos Aires. The British regulars expected an easy fight but their opponents, a colonial militia, defended their city street by street. The coherence of the attack soon broke up, and it was the British who surrendered. This victory so stimulated the colonists' self-confidence that they soon broke from Spain, fighting a long war of independence in which Britain, their former enemy, became an ally. In gratitude the new Republic of Argentina named a main square in Buenos Aires the Plaza Britannica. British investment poured into Argentina, first into cattle ranching and then into railways, and the younger sons of the British aristocracy and gentry came down to Buenos Aires and married into the Argentine elite. They sent their children to Argentine versions of English public schools, and many later studied at Oxford and Cambridge. They also bred horses that did well in British race meetings, and played polo to a very high standard. By the early 1980s the Anglo-Argentine elite boasted relatives of the Princess of Wales and the Duchess of York; the Chairman of the Conservative Party, Lord Vesty, visited Buenos Aires regularly to oversee his vast business investments, and many British cavalry officers came out at least once a year to try to win back polo trophies.

Relations between Britain and Argentina were bedevilled by only one problem. Britain and Spain had both claimed the Falkland Islands, and along with independence in 1820 Argentina had inherited the Spanish rights. In 1831 the American frigate *Lemington* had removed the small number of Argentine settlers, after they had been in dispute with American sealers. Two years later the British reasserted their rights and established a colony. The population grew slowly, peaked at about 2,400 in 1931, and then declined slowly to about 2,000 by 1980. During this century and a half the islanders developed a distinctive accent and a distinctive, but still very British, culture. Though remote, they had been touched many times by world events – in 1914, for example, when several Islanders had lost their lives in the Battle of the Falkland

The South Atlantic: Argentine and British territorial claims

URUGUAY

Buenos Aires

ARGENTINA

1. Argentina base since 1976.
2. Claimed by Britain, Argentina and Chile.

Falkland Islands
(Malvinas)

South Georgia

CHILE

60'S

South Sandwich
Islands
1

ANTARCTIC
TERRITORY
2

N

0   500 miles
0   1,000 km

South Pole

1. Argentine base on South Thule since 1976
2. Territorial claims put forward by Britain, Argentina and Chile

Islands, and again in 1939 when HMS *Exeter* put into Stanley for repairs during the hunt for the *Graf Spee*. They had also played a role in the last great age of Antarctic exploration, and in the early 1980s old islanders would recall meeting Ernest Shackleton and Roald Amundsen. Life was hard and simple, not unlike that enjoyed by the natives of the Outer Hebrides. By 1980 some families had been on the islands for more than five generations, and were to all intents and purposes natives of the Falklands.

Unfortunately Argentina had never relinquished its claim on the Falkland Islands, reviving it in 1910 and again in 1927, when it was extended to include not only the islands themselves but dependencies administered by the British governor from the Falklands: the island of South Georgia and the South Sandwich Islands. After joining the United Nations after the Second World War, Argentina lobbied patiently to have the Falklands recognised as a decolonisation issue, in accordance with United Nations General Assembly Resolution 114 of 1945. Years of diplomatic manoeuvre paid off in 1965 with General Assembly Resolution 2065, which called on Britain and Argentina to negotiate 'bearing in mind Resolution 114 and the interests [not the wishes] of the islanders'.

Negotiations began in 1966 and dragged on until 1980. Officials at the Foreign Office quickly decided that the 'interests' of the islanders, and Britain's interests in South America, lay in transferring sovereignty of the Falklands to Argentina as quickly as possible. To this end they discouraged investment in the islands and signed a communications agreement with Argentina, which made the Falklands dependent on Argentina for weekly air flights. Unfortunately for the Foreign Office, the Falkland Islands Company (founded in 1851 and now controlled by the British company Coalite), which owned nearly half the islands, and the Falkland Islands Committee, a parliamentary lobby group created by members of the Falkland Islands Executive Council in Britain in 1968, had sufficient

political power to prevent an outright handover. This power increased during the 1970s with the beginnings of the 'Dirty War' in Argentina and the military coup of 1976, which placed the country under a succession of military juntas. In 1979, in a renewed attempt to obviate opposition, the new Foreign Secretary, Lord Carrington, a career diplomat, devised a lease-back agreement as a possible solution, where Argentina would be given sovereignty in return for Britain maintaining day-to-day administration during a long lease period. This solution appeared to be acceptable to the leaders in Buenos Aires, but when it came before the House of Commons on 2 December 1980, was roundly condemned.

There was now an impasse. After 14 years of negotiations Argentine diplomats had apparently run into a brick wall. And yet other departments in Whitehall began activities that suggested that Britain had washed its hands of the islands. The Home Office decided that the 1981 Nationality Act would not include an exception for Falkland Islanders, most of whom were now deprived of their automatic right to British citizenship. Whitehall also announced that the future of the British Antarctic Survey Base at Grytviken in South Georgia was under review. The Ministry of Defence announced the results of a major Defence Review, which recommended selling off or scrapping about one-third of the Royal Navy's surface fleet, including the light carriers *Hermes* and *Invincible*, and the Landing Ship Dock *Intrepid*. There was also widespread speculation in the press of plans to abolish the Royal Marines. However, the announcement that had the greatest impact on the Junta was the MoD's decision to withdraw the Antarctic Protection Vessel *Endurance*, and not replace her. This ship not only had a sophisticated intelligence-gathering capability, but was also a highly visible symbol of Britain's determination to retain its interests in the South Atlantic. When these straws in the wind were taken in combination, there was only one conclusion the Junta could reach – that Britain had decided to abandon its territories in the South Atlantic, and would shortly lack the capacity to defend them, even if she were to change her mind.

All Argentines wanted the return of the Malvinas, but it was a *cause célèbre* for the Argentine navy. When a junta ousted the government of Isabelita Peron in November 1976, the navy was given the green light to test Britain's resolve. Within a few weeks Argentine warships attempted to arrest the British research ship *Shackleton* south of the Falklands for sailing in Argentine territorial waters. Later that year the navy raised the Argentine flag on South Thule in the South Sandwich Islands and established a small scientific station, which was so remote that Britain chose to ignore it. Provocative naval manoeuvres in November the following year elicited a more robust response, with Britain dispatching a task force of a submarine and two frigates to the South Atlantic.

On 16 December 1981 a new junta ousted the government of General Viola. It was headed by General Leopoldo Galtieri, a large,

amiable soldier, politically naive and reputedly extremely fond of the bottle. Galtieri was dominated intellectually by the naval member of the Junta, the Commander-in-Chief of the navy, Admiral Jorge Anaya. Unusually amongst the Argentine elite, Anaya was an Anglophobe, a year spent in London as a naval attaché having given him a profound dislike of Britain and all things British. It was rumoured that he had only agreed to support Galtieri's coup on condition that the general allowed the navy to push ahead with schemes for removing Britain not just from the Falklands, but from her other territories in the South Atlantic. The third member of the Junta, a senior air force officer, Brigadier General Basilio Lami Dozo, was more cautious, but still gave Anaya guarded support.

The Junta. Galtieri, Lami Dozo and Anaya pose for a photo call. Anaya made his support for the takeover on 16 December 1981 conditional on the agreement of Lami Dozo and Galtieri to retake the Malvinas. (Gamma)

The Atlantic area of operations

Since early December the naval staff had been planning two operations in the greatest secrecy: Project Alpha, a plan for the clandestine establishment of an Argentine presence on South Georgia; and Operation Azul, a blueprint for a full-scale invasion of the Falklands. As with many highly secret preparations, co-ordination between Alpha and Azul soon broke down. Azul was the responsibility of Vice Admiral Juan Jose Lombardo, Chief of Naval Operations, and involved the employment of all of Argentina's major warships, including the aircraft carrier, and about 3,000 troops from the Argentine marines and the elite Buzo Tactico, the Argentine special forces. Lombardo finished the first version of the plan around 15 March 1982. The invasion was scheduled for the period mid-May to mid-July, the preferred date being 9 July, Argentina's Independence Day. This would be after the departure of *Endurance* from the South Atlantic, which would very much reduce the danger of detection in the final phases, and would reduce the opposition (*Endurance* carried two missile-armed Wasp

helicopters) to a detachment of some 30 Royal Marines at Port Stanley. In addition, it was the middle of the southern winter, when weather conditions would render large-scale naval movements and military operations problematical, in the unlikely event that Britain chose to respond.

Meanwhile the first stage of Alpha had gone into operation in December 1981, when the navy landed an Argentine scrap-metal merchant, Constantino Davidoff, and a party of 41 workers at Leith on the north-west coast of South Georgia, ostensibly to conduct a preliminary survey of a derelict whaling station with a view to its demolition. Davidoff pointedly refused to report to the British base at Grytviken, 30 miles to the east, to have his entry visas stamped, a breach of procedure that

Endurance at Grytviken on the northern coast of South Georgia, October 1981. The Antarctic Protection Vessel was not just a visible symbol of Britain's determination to protect her South Atlantic dependencies, she also carried sophisticated intelligence-gathering equipment and was regarded in Argentina as a 'spy ship'. The British decision to scrap *Endurance* triggered the crisis. (Gamma)

eventually elicited a protest from London. On 9 March 1982 Davidoff and his party returned to Leith aboard the Argentine transport *Bahia Buen Suceso*, once more refused to comply with formal entry procedures, and this time raised the Argentine flag.

In Buenos Aires the British ambassador made light of Davidoff's activities. A very different attitude was taken by the governor of the Falklands, Rex Hunt, and his old friend Captain Nick Barker, the commander of *Endurance*, which had put into Stanley on 19 March. Both men believed the Argentine presence at Leith was a provocation designed to test British resolve, and Hunt managed to convince the Foreign Office to allow him to send *Endurance* back to South Georgia with a party of 22 Royal Marines, who would either defend Grytviken or eject the Argentines from Leith.

Battling against a Force 10 gale, *Endurance* took four days to reach South Georgia, anchoring at Grytviken on the morning of Wednesday 24 March. By then the 'Davidoff Incident' had been widely covered in the British press, and debated in the House of Commons. Broadsheets and tabloids alike revelled in the drama of *Endurance* ploughing through mountainous seas to eject an Argentine landing on South Georgia. More importantly, there was widespread speculation that *Endurance* would not be alone for long, with rumours of the actual and imminent departure of nuclear submarines to back up the activities of the Antarctic Protection Vessel, stories which the junior Foreign Office Minister, Henry Luce, described as 'unhelpful'. Five days later the British media carried the story that the nuclear submarine *Superb* had left Gibraltar on Thursday 25 March for the South Atlantic. It had not, but on the day the story appeared (Monday 29 March) three nuclear submarines had indeed been ordered to the Falklands. However, it was now too late to deter Argentina.

The Junta met on 25 March. Anaya, convinced by the storm in the British media that the South Atlantic would be awash with

British nuclear submarines on or before 10 April, demanded that Operation Azul go ahead immediately. Working around the clock, Lombardo and his staff produced a modified plan codenamed Operation Rosario. On 28 March Task Force 40, the Falklands invasion force, steamed out of the Argentine naval base of Puerto Belgrano. It consisted of the ex-American tank landing ship *Cabo San Antonio*, loaded with 20 American-built amphibious landing vehicles, and the transport *Isla de los Estados*. Together they had carried some 900 troops, drawn mainly from the 2nd Marine Infantry

An Argentine Amtrack rolls through the streets of Stanley early on 2 April 1982. The soldier was posing for the cameras but there is no doubt that his enthusiasm was genuine. (Gamma)

Battalion, based in Puerto Belgrano, and the Buzo Tactico. Gunfire support was provided by the destroyers *Hercules* and *Santisima Trinidad*, and the frigates *Drummond* and *Granville*. To the north the aircraft carrier *Veinticinco de Mayo*, escorted by the remainder of the Argentine navy, provided distant cover.

Britain's giant electronic listening station, GCHQ Cheltenham, had picked up Argentine radio traffic on 26 March which suggested a large-scale exercise was under way. Five days later, the evening of Wednesday 31 March, Cheltenham intercepted a message to the Argentine submarine *Santa Fe*, ordering it to land reconnaissance troops of the Buzo Tactico on the beach at Mullett Creek to the west of Port Stanley in the early hours of 2 April. Governor Hunt was alerted immediately. In the few hours that remained, he and Major Mike Norman, the commander of the Royal Marine detachment, determined to make sure the Argentines experienced something more than token resistance. Thanks to the invasion occurring during a relief of the garrison, Norman had 68 Marines, double the usual number, along with 25 members of the Local Defence Force and

Buenos Aires, Friday 2 April 1982. An immense crowd estimated at more than 200,000 packs the Plaza de Mayo to celebrate the liberation of the Malvinas. The Junta hoped that their adventurous foreign policy would distract the people from problems at home and for a time they succeeded. (Gamma)

The picture that made war inevitable. Pointing their rifles Argentine special forces make Royal Marine prisoners lie on their stomachs. Within a few hours this image had been radio-photographed all over the world and helped stir up the public storm which was to break in Britain. (Gamma)

11 sailors from *Endurance* who had remained in Stanley when their ship sailed to South Georgia. Norman fortified Government House on the eastern edge of Stanley as best he could, and positioned the remainder of his force to cover likely landing beaches. The Argentines struck shortly after 0600 on 2 April. A platoon of the Buzo Tactico came ashore to the north-east and shot up and destroyed the empty Marine barracks at Moody Brook, while another group attempted to storm Government House, and were driven off by the Marines' heavy fire. In the meantime, Marine positions to the west opened up with machine guns and light anti-tank weapons on Argentine Amtracks as they came ashore, destroying at least one, and damaging several others. Hugely outnumbered, the Marines fell back into Stanley or withdrew towards Government House. For the next hour the streets of the town echoed to bouts of firing, which became increasingly sporadic as the Marines and Local Defence Force ran short of ammunition, until the firing stopped at about 0830. The Argentines now moved Amtracks up to Government House, the last centre of resistance, and surrounded it.

Facing annihilation Governor Hunt surrendered at 0930.

Meanwhile the Argentine frigate *Guerrico* had arrived at Leith on South Georgia, which was already occupied by Argentine Marines and sailors. On the morning of 3 April an Argentine Puma and two Alouettes attempted to land troops at Grytviken, but ran into heavy fire from the Royal Marine detachment, the Puma being badly hit and forced to crash land, killing most on board. The *Guerrico* now appeared at the narrow entrance to the harbour, but retreated hastily to the outer harbour after being hit by bursts

'The Iron Lady'. Taken in mid-April 1982, the picture is a study of strain and determination. The Junta had assumed that Britain's first female prime minister would hesitate before plunging into war, and lived to regret their miscalculation. (Gamma)

of machine gun fire and three anti-tank rockets in quick succession, one of which holed her hull. Safely out of range of the Marines' small arms, the *Guerrico* began to bombard their positions with her 100 mm gun, while Argentine troops, now disembarked from the helicopters, moved in on the Marines' flanks. Having done much more than could reasonably be expected of them, the Marines' 22-year-old commander, Lt Keith Mills, ordered his men to cease fire.

British territory had been invaded, but it was by no means axiomatic that Britain would respond by sending a task force to the South Atlantic. Initial assessments on the evening of 31 March from the Joint Intelligence Committee, and from a variety of other interested parties, argued that a military operation conducted 8,000 miles from base, in deteriorating weather conditions and against a numerous and well-equipped enemy was problematical, to say the least. By 1 April a consensus was emerging that the response would have to rely on Britain's diplomacy, though Mrs Thatcher, the prime minister, was deeply concerned that the public and parliamentary storm that was certain to greet the news of the invasion would damage her government beyond repair. She revelled in the title 'The Iron Lady', bestowed on her by Soviet commentators, and felt that more was expected of her in a time of crisis than might be expected of a male Prime Minister. Even if her government were to survive, she would be unlikely to last long as premier or party leader.

Unfortunately for the Prime Minister, the key man in such a crisis, the Chief of the Defence Staff, Admiral Sir Terrence Lewin, was hurrying back from a conference in New Zealand. In his absence, the First Sea Lord, Admiral Sir Henry Leach, sought out Mrs Thatcher in the House of Commons on the evening of 1 April. The admiral contradicted all the assessments she had received so far. He agreed that an attempt to retake the islands would be difficult and dangerous, but thought it was not impossible, and that in any event she had no choice. Perhaps moved by the setting, the place where statesmen over the centuries had dealt with so many desperate crises, Leach rose to the occasion. He told the Prime Minister that if she did not send a task force Britain would soon be a very different country, a nation whose word counted for very little in the affairs of the world. Leach's appeal to simple patriotism struck the right chord. Shortly after midnight on 1/2 April, orders began pouring out of the Ministry of Defence to warships, the Royal Marines and to squadrons of the Royal Air Force.

When the news of the Argentine invasion reached Britain late on Friday 2 April a storm of public indignation and anger broke, much greater than anything Mrs Thatcher had anticipated. Britain's national morale was low. There was the long-term problem of the steady decline from great power status. But there were also more immediate problems. Only nine months earlier the worst urban riots of the twentieth century had torn through more than 40 British cities and towns, while in January unemployment passed the three million mark for the first time since the Great Depression of the early 1930s. It now seemed to many that Britain had hit rock bottom. A South American dictatorship had invaded British territory, and now its soldiers, amongst whom were men who were widely believed to be torturers and murderers, lorded it over British people. The first pictures of the invasion that were radio-photo'd around the world showed Royal Marines being forced to lie face down in the dirt, and reinforced the sense of national outrage. Most British people had never felt anything like this anger before, but there were those amongst the very old who said that they had – it reminded them very much of the summer of 1914. On Saturday 3 April in an emergency session of the House of Commons Mrs Thatcher and her ministers faced a storm of criticism. Her Foreign Secretary, Lord Carrington, and two of his junior ministers chose to resign, but Mrs Thatcher rode it out, announcing that if diplomacy failed Operation Corporate, the forceful removal of the Argentines, would succeed.

Race to the islands: Argentina and Britain deploy their forces

Britain's official position in April 1982 was that she preferred to resolve the crisis through diplomatic negotiation, and would only employ the task force if peaceful means failed. In fact, it was the exigencies of military operations that set the timetable, not the requirements of the diplomats. This is not to say there were not elements within

HMS *Invincible* steams out of Portsmouth on 5 April 1982. Her departure, along with that of *Hermes*, sent a signal to the Junta that Britain was preparing to back diplomacy with force. (Rex Features)

Britain who were working desperately for a peaceful outcome. The new Foreign Secretary, Francis Pym, laboured earnestly for a compromise, though it was rumoured within some sections of the Conservative Party that his real purpose was to inflict political damage on his arch rival, the Prime Minister. Al Haig, the US Secretary of State, an old friend of Pym's, conducted a frenetic 'shuttle diplomacy', which attempted to address both Argentine and British

requirements, and in the end satisfied neither. Mrs Thatcher was much more in tune with the mood of the British people than was Francis Pym and other Conservative grandees. She sensed that they were not much interested in a peaceful compromise and nor was she. Nothing less than an Argentine departure from the islands with British sovereignty fully restored would do, and this was a price she strongly suspected the Junta could not afford to pay.

A ghost that had haunted a generation of British Prime Ministers whenever they considered military action was that of the Suez Canal debacle of 1956. Determined not to repeat the mistakes of Anthony Eden, Mrs Thatcher consulted two previous Prime Ministers, the Earl of Stockton (Harold Macmillan) and Lord Callaghan, who told her to keep political and military activity tightly co-ordinated. She therefore decided to establish an inner committee to manage the crisis, which was quickly dubbed the 'War Cabinet'. Chaired by the Prime Minister, the War Cabinet included Francis Pym, Defence Secretary John Nott, Home Secretary William Whitelaw, Chancellor of the Exchequer Geoffrey Howe and Chairman of the Conservative Party Cecil Parkinson. It had as its professional advisers a team of key civil servants and service chiefs, led by the Chief of the Defence Staff Sir Terence Lewin. The composition of the War Cabinet meant that the diplomatic and domestic political ramifications of any military action could be quickly assessed and appropriate instructions issued. Likewise, British diplomacy could be used to increase the likelihood of a peaceful solution rather than the avoidance of a military solution.

Thus the main thrust of Britain's diplomatic effort was not to effect a compromise but to place Argentina in the wrong, to isolate her, and to keep her isolated. Argentina's Foreign Ministry attempted to respond, but its efforts were feeble and poorly co-ordinated. It was a most unequal competition between a heavyweight diplomatic machine which had been playing power politics on the world stage for more than four centuries, and a foreign ministry that could just about manage relations with a few of its Latin American neighbours. While Mrs Thatcher was bearing the wrath of the House of Commons on 3 April, Britain's ambassador to the United Nations, Sir Anthony Parsons, engineered the passage of Resolution 502 through the Security Council, which stressed the illegitimacy of the use of force and called for an immediate withdrawal of Argentine forces. On the same day the Foreign Office secured France's agreement to halt the export to Argentina of Exocet missiles, Super Etendard Aircraft and engines for Pucara aircraft, all of which would seriously compromise Argentina's military capability. The impact of this ban was extended on 9 April, when Britain managed to secure an EEC trade embargo on Argentina for one month, with an option to extend the embargo further.

The great diplomatic prize was winning the support of the United States. Argentina had placed her hopes in the close personal relationship that had developed between Galtieri and some of the American military, which included Al Haig, and in the support of Jeane Kirkpatrick, the US ambassador to the United Nations, and a friend of Argentine Foreign Minister Costa Mendez. In fact, there was not the slightest prospect of the United States supporting Argentina against Great Britain. It was not merely that America and Britain shared a history and a culture and subscribed to identical values. With the Cold War entering what proved to be its final and most dangerous phase, a major ally such as Britain would inevitably be regarded as more important than a relatively remote country in the southern hemisphere. US Secretary of Defense Caspar Weinberger let it be known that he wanted the military to 'give the Brits every possible assistance, but not, under any circumstances, to be caught doing so'. Weinberger's decision was of the utmost importance. Without American logistic support, most of which was channelled through Ascension Island, the operation would have taken much longer, and would undoubtedly have been compromised by the onset of the southern winter.

With this intense diplomatic activity going on in the background, the first elements of the task force, the carriers *Hermes* and *Invincible*, sailed from Portsmouth on 5 April. Over the next few weeks British ports saw many departures, most spectacularly that of *Canberra* carrying 40 and 45 Commando of the Royal Marines and 3rd Battalion of the Parachute Regiment, all of which attracted immense media interest. The emphasis was on speed, because these highly publicised sailings were

designed to send a strong message to Buenos Aires and as a result the loading had often been chaotic. The actual assembly of the task force took place in mid-April, as ships rendezvoused in the Georgetown Roads off Ascension Island, a 3,000-foot volcanic cone almost exactly halfway between the British Isles and the Falklands. In 1943 American engineers had constructed Wideawake airfield on a steep lava flow at the foot of the volcano, and this had since been developed into a major base. British servicemen who

flew in recalled that Ascension, its barren volcanic crags festooned with aerials and satellite dishes, reminded them of Tracey Island, the secret base of Thunderbirds, a children's television programme popular in the 1960s.

The stop at Ascension was essential, for it enabled the British to organise not just the shipping but also a command chain. As this was an 'out of area' operation dependent on the Royal Navy the Commander-in-Chief Fleet, Admiral Sir John Fieldhouse, based at

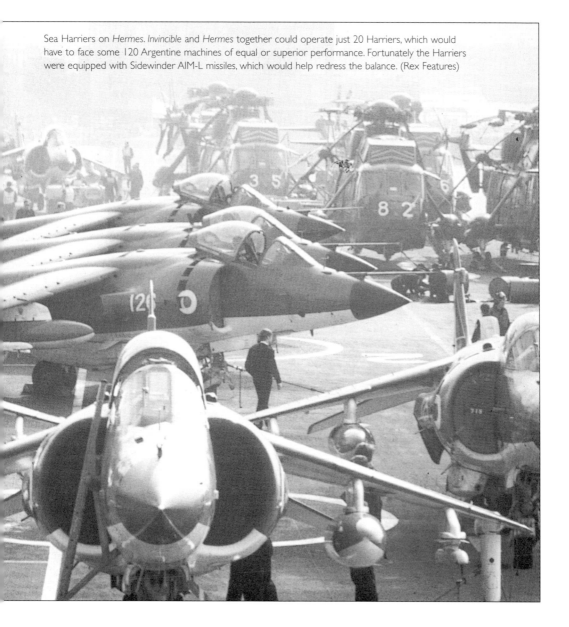

Sea Harriers on *Hermes*. *Invincible* and *Hermes* together could operate just 20 Harriers, which would have to face some 120 Argentine machines of equal or superior performance. Fortunately the Harriers were equipped with Sidewinder AIM-L missiles, which would help redress the balance. (Rex Features)

Northwood, was designated Task Force Commander, reporting directly to Admiral Lewin, the CDS. The commander of the Royal Marines, Major General Jeremy Moore, was appointed Fieldhouse's land forces deputy. Under Fieldhouse were the operational commanders: Rear Admiral John 'Sandy' Woodward, appointed to command the carriers and surface warships, Commodore Michael Clapp, given command of the amphibious ships, including *Fearless* and *Intrepid*, and Brigadier Julian Thompson, commanding the Landing Task Group. A major problem with this arrangement was the absence of an on-the-spot theatre commander to co-ordinate the activities of the three operational commanders with Northwood, but this was not apparent at the time. Another difficulty was caused by Fieldhouse's insistence that the submarines take orders from Northwood, rather than from Woodward.

The first problem the commanders had to face was planning the logistics, for they all knew that the key to Operation Corporate was the ability of the Royal Navy and the Royal Air Force to construct and maintain an 8,000-mile supply line that would be capable of sustaining military forces in the South Atlantic. An air bridge from Britain to Wideawake would have been impossible if the US Air Force had not handed over 12.5 million gallons of highly refined aviation fuel. With this, the 54 Hercules C-130s of 24, 30, 47 and 70 squadrons and the 13 VC 10s of 10 squadron, supplemented by three Belfast strategic freighters and a number of Boeing 707s, managed 2,500 flights between the beginning of April and the middle of June, which delivered some 30,000 tons of freight and several thousand personnel. Equally important was the work of the helicopters, which allowed chaotically stowed supplies to be sorted out, cross-decked, and combat loaded. All this involved 10,600 helicopter movements. The busiest day was 16 April, when 300 fixed wing and helicopter flights were recorded, making Wideawake the world's busiest airport.

The most important shipping movements in the early part of the campaign were not the highly publicised departures of the aircraft carriers and the *Canberra*, but the sailing of nine Royal Fleet Auxiliary oil tankers, soon supplemented by another 14 tankers taken up from trade, for without these ships the task force would be unable to proceed. Beginning on 2 April the Defence Operations Movement Staff (DOMS) in the Ministry of Defence contracted and requisitioned 68 ships from 33 different companies, which ranged from the luxury liners like *Canberra* and the *QE2* to North

Men of 2 Para, about to board buses to take them to Portsmouth and the North Sea Ferry *Norland*. Once in the Falklands the Sterling sub-machine guns the men carried were quickly abandoned in favour of FN30 rifles captured from the Argentines. (Gamma)

Sea tug boats. In addition, the Royal Fleet Auxiliary provided 16 cargo transports, bringing the total number of ships sustaining the task force to 84, about the size of a large Second World War convoy.

All these transports were required to keep the warships of the task force, two aircraft carriers, five destroyers, 11 frigates and three nuclear submarines, operating in the South Atlantic for just six weeks. The submarines, *Conqueror*, *Spartan* and *Splendid*, capable of 25 knots submerged, raced ahead to blockade the Falklands, and to seek out and destroy Argentine submarines. When they arrived some days later the carriers would employ their 20 Sea Harrier aircraft to attack Port Stanley airfield and other Argentine bases. Although the Fleet Air Arm pilots were supremely confident of their ability to engage in successful air combat with Argentine Mirage IIICs, trial combats then being conducted between RAF Harriers and

French Mirages suggested that the Mirage was the superior aircraft. This disparity was no longer a cause for concern. Ever since the Israeli Air Force had been shot out of the sky by Egyptian and Syrian anti-aircraft missile systems at the beginning of the Yom Kippur War in October 1973, it had been an article of faith that air superiority could be attained by ground- or sea-based missiles. Nowhere was this belief stronger than in the Royal Navy, whose destroyers and frigates bristled with Sea Cats, Sea Wolfs and Sea Darts. Royal Navy ships were also equipped with ship-to-ship Exocet missiles, which would be more than adequate to deal with a threat from any Argentine warships. It was known that the Argentines were also acquiring Exocets, but it was believed that none were

Brigadier General Mario Menendez arrives in the Malvinas. Menendez's role was to be that of governor, but he was soon faced with organising a defence against invasion. He was a competent soldier but the Argentine army was a very imperfect instrument. (Gamma)

men) of 3 Commando Brigade, Royal Marines, would spearhead the assault. The 2nd and 3rd Battalions of the Parachute Regiment, possibly the only troops of the army at that time whose general standard of training and fitness was equal to that of the Marines, were attached to 3 Brigade, along with two troops of light tanks from the Blues and Royals, and Air Defence Regiments from the Royal Artillery. Squadrons of 22 Special Air Service, who would conduct reconnaissance missions and carry out raids, were also aboard the transports. All told, the assault force numbered just 7,000 men, who were amongst the fittest, the best trained and the most highly motivated of any soldiers in the world.

In Argentina the euphoria that had greeted the 'liberation' of the Malvinas, steadily gave way to disbelief and alarm, as the magnitude of British preparations for war became ever more apparent. Brigadier General Mario Menendez had arrived in Stanley on 7 April to assume the role of governor, not of garrison commander, but he soon found himself overseeing a desperate build-up of men and materiel. The navy devoted all five of its transports, and also chartered ships from Argentina's national shipping line. In all nine ships displacing a total of 80,000 tons were loaded, of which eight successfully completed the voyage before British submarines reached the area. Argentina supplemented shipping with an airbridge. Between 2 and 29 April the air force's nine Hercules C-130 transports assisted by a small number of Fokker F28s, Navy Lockheed Electras and Argentine National Airlines Boeing 737s and BAC 111s flew around the clock. A total of 500 landings were made at Stanley airfield, bringing 10,700 men and 5,500 tons of supplies, mainly weapons and ammunition. Movement by air meant that heavy equipment or equipment deemed

in operation before France withdrew technical support. British warships also had guns, and these would be used to bombard Argentine positions prior to a landing.

The object of all this air and sea activity was to put a landing force ashore in the Falklands. As this was an amphibious operation it was axiomatic that the three Commandos (40, 42 and 45, each of 500 non-essential such as tents, cooking utensils and entrenching tools were removed from units and sent by the few merchant ships that dared the exclusion zone. On average, three weeks were to elapse before units were married up with their equipment but in many cases equipment did not reach the islands at all.

The first reinforcements to arrive came from the 10 Infantry Brigade under Brigadier General Oscar Joffre, reinforced by 3 Infantry Brigade under Brigadier General Omar Parada on 24 April. Unlike the all-volunteer British army, the Argentine army was composed of conscripts. An early problem was the need to replace the January 1982 intake of 19-year-old conscripts (the class of 1963) who filled Parada's and Joffre's brigades with the recently discharged 20-year-old 'veterans' of the class of 1962. This process resulted in some disorganisation. The only units that escaped this were Argentina's Marine regiments, which, unlike the army, inducted one-sixth of the conscripts they required every two months. Thus at any one time the great majority of a Marine regiment had completed at least its basic training. About a

month after the landing Argentina had deployed some 13,000 men to the islands, which comprised eight infantry and two Marine regiments, an Argentine regiment being equivalent to a British battalion. The army had also sent a number of artillery units, which could field 42 105mm and four 155mm guns and 23 quick-firing anti-aircraft guns. These were supplemented by a number of Roland and Tiger Cat surface-to-air missile launchers and heavy machine gun units, which boasted about 40 12.7mm guns. Argentina decided against deploying heavy armour, but did send a light reconnaissance squadron with 27 armoured cars.

It was easy enough to pour troops and equipment into the islands, but less easy to arrive at a coherent scheme of defence that made best use of Argentina's air and naval forces, as well as her land forces. On 7 April Argentina attempted to create a degree of inter-service co-operation by establishing the South Atlantic Operational Theatre under Vice Admiral Lombardo. On the islands there was an unseemly squabble for dominance between Menendez and the senior representatives of the navy and the air force,

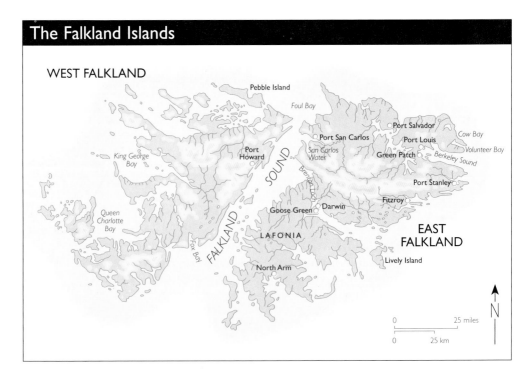

The Falkland Islands

WEST FALKLAND

Pebble Island

Foul Bay

Port Salvador

Cow Bay

Port San Carlos

Port Louis

Volunteer Bay

Port Howard

San Carlos Water

Green Patch

Berkeley Sound

King George Bay

SOUND

Port Stanley

Fitzroy

Queen Charlotte Bay

Goose Green

Darwin

LAFONIA

EAST FALKLAND

Lively Island

Fox Bay

North Arm

0   25 miles

0   25 km

N

Rear-Admiral Edgardo Otero and Brigadier General Luis Castellano. The manoeuvring came to a formal conclusion on 26 April when Menendez appointed himself as head of the Malvinas Joint Command, a usurpation which won the approval of the Junta. The conflict now became internecine, and was complicated by the fact that Menendez was junior to his two army brigadier generals, Joffre and Parada, both of whom tended to treat his orders as suggestions. By the end of April five brigadier generals and a rear-admiral had set up their headquarters in Stanley, each with their own not inconsiderable staff, comprising, by one calculation, about 3,000 of the 13,000 men Argentina had sent to the Falklands. To make matters worse, any hope of developing a coherent defence plan collapsed after 19 April when individual members of the Junta dealt with Menendez directly, each representing their own service rather than the armed forces as a whole. Admiral Anaya visited Menendez on 19 April, Lami Dozo on 20 April, the Chief of Staff General Cristino Nicholaides on 21 April, and Galtieri on 22 April.

When the shooting started Argentina's first line of defence would be the Fuerza Aerea Argentina (FAA) (air force), with some 120 high-performance combat jet aircraft, more than enough to overwhelm the Royal Navy's defensive systems. The British feared that the FAA would extend Stanley's 4,700-foot airfield with steel matting so that it would be long enough to allow Mirages, Daggers and Skyhawks to operate from it. Argentina had ample supplies of steel matting and enough time to ship it to Stanley, but when air force engineers studied the practicalities they decided it would be too difficult to sustain high-performance jet aircraft from such a primitive field. Super-Etendards and Daggers required specialised fuel storage facilities, workshops capable of maintaining and repairing sophisticated avionics and weapons systems, and hardened bunkers to protect the aircraft from British attack. High performance aircraft based at Stanley without these

Argentine air bases

facilities would be essentially single-shot weapons. If they did not destroy the British in their first operation the British would almost certainly destroy them.

This decision meant that the FAA's first line combat aircraft would be forced to operate from bases in Argentina. Skyhawk A-4Bs and Mirage III Es were deployed to Rio Gallegos in the south-east of Patagonia; Skyhawk A-4Cs and Daggers were based at San Julian, 180 miles to the north; long-range Canberra bombers would fly from Trelew another 450 miles further north, while Daggers were sent to Rio Grande on the north-east coast of Tierra del Fuego, along with the navy's Skyhawk A-4Qs and Super Etendards. By the end of April about

Douglas A-4C Skyhawks. The Skyhawk was the workhorse of the Argentine air force. Although first in service in 1957 the Skyhawk's performance was comparable to the Harrier. Argentina lost 19 of her 60 Skyhawks, and 17 pilots were killed, but Skyhawks sank three British warships and two auxiliaries. (Gamma)

80 machines were in the southern bases, approximately two-thirds of Argentina's first line air strength. Air operations were to be controlled from a command set up at Comodoro Rivadavia air base on the coast of central Patagonia, which would rely on information supplied by a long-range Westinghouse AN/TPS-43 F radar set up in Port Stanley. Most of the bases were more than 400 miles from the islands, which severely limited the time aircraft could spend in the area. In-flight refuelling could extend the range, but the FAA had only three tanker aircraft, and only the 60 Skyhawks and the five Super Etendards had an in-flight refuelling capability.

Thanks to Argentina's counter-insurgency operations, the FAA was lavishly equipped with Pucara IA-58 ground attack aircraft, about 30 of which were flown to Stanley and to the airfield at the Falkland's second settlement, Darwin–Goose Green. The navy reinforced the AAF, sending six

Aermacchi MB.339A advanced jet trainers converted to a ground attack role to Stanley and six Beechcraft T-34 C-1 Turbo Mentor trainers, equipped with a variety of weapons pods, to operate from a grass runway on Pebble Island, which the Argentines christened Calderon Naval Air Station. The aircraft based in the Falklands, while lacking the capacity to attack the task force directly, could supplement the attacks of mainland-based jets. In addition, the Argentine army deployed a number of light transport aircraft to the islands, and 27 helicopters, including three heavy-lift Chinooks.

The Argentine navy, with four submarines an aircraft carrier, and a number of Exocet-equipped warships, also had the capability to attack the task force while it was well to the north of the islands. But like the FAA, the naval high command decided that a deployment too far forward risked playing to British strengths. The Royal Navy, for example, was the world leader in anti-submarine warfare, and any attempt by Argentina's four boats to attack the Task Force as it sailed south of Ascension was likely to end in their loss. It was felt the same fate would befall any Argentine surface units, particularly old ships like the aircraft carrier and the cruiser *Belgrano*, which ventured in range of the Task Force without the benefit of land-based air support. The navy decided to wait until the British were heavily involved in an air–sea engagement to hit them with simultaneous surface and submarine attacks.

If the FAA and the navy failed to prevent a British landing, it would be up to Menendez's young conscripts to defeat them in a land battle. Menendez had too few troops to prevent a landing at some point on the heavily indented coastline of the islands which were about 4,000 square miles in area, about half the size of Wales. He sent 800 men to Port Howard and another 900 to Fox Bay to establish a presence on West Falkland Island, with a detachment of 120 to Pebble Island, and about 1,200 to Darwin–Goose Green. Menendez knew that the vital ground was Port Stanley with its airfield and harbour. If he could hold this area long enough the British logistic system would inevitably break down, and they would be forced to withdraw from the South Atlantic. He therefore concentrated the bulk of his forces in an all round defence, with the 25th, 6th and 3rd regiments dug in to cover the beaches from the airfield to Mullett Creek, while the 5th Marines and the 4th and 7th regiments were dug into the hills and mountains to the west of Stanley, Mt Harriet, Two Sisters, Tumbledown, Mt Longdon and Wireless Ridge. Menendez placed most of his artillery in and around

Argentine troops dig in on the beach near Mullett Creek, south-west of Port Stanley. They were well equipped for cold weather with quilted parkas bought from the Israeli Defence Force, and Argentine-manufactured boots very much superior to the DMS boots worn by the British. However, many troops came from the sub-tropical north of Argentina, and found the conditions of the Falklands winter increasingly trying. (Department of War Studies, Sandhurst)

Stanley, from where it could support the forces on the beaches or in the mountains, and where it would be protected from British attack by the proximity of the civilian population. His plan was to fight an attritional battle from fixed defences, which was subsequently much criticised, but which suited admirably the capabilities of the soldiers he had at his disposal.

'Gotcha!' The sinking of the *Belgrano*

For the first three weeks of April the Junta clung to the belief that Britain was engaged in an enormous game of bluff, and that the dispute would be settled by negotiation. On 22 April Francis Pym flew to Washington to consult with Al Haig, and two days later a new peace proposal was waiting for Costa Mendez when he arrived in the United States

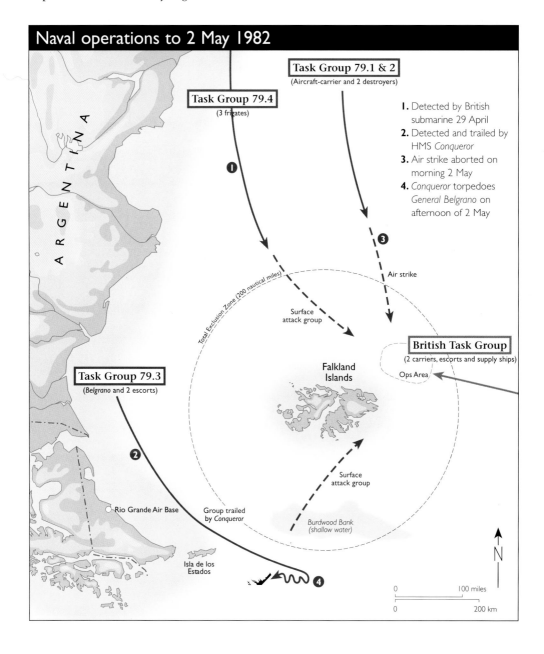

Naval operations to 2 May 1982

Task Group 79.1 & 2
(Aircraft-carrier and 2 destroyers)

Task Group 79.4
(3 frigates)

1. Detected by British submarine 29 April
2. Detected and trailed by HMS *Conqueror*
3. Air strike aborted on morning 2 May
4. *Conqueror* torpedoes *General Belgrano* on afternoon of 2 May

Total Exclusion Zone (200 nautical miles)

Surface attack group

Air strike

British Task Group
(2 carriers, escorts and supply ships)

Falkland Islands

Ops Area

Task Group 79.3
(*Belgrano* and 2 escorts)

Surface attack group

Rio Grande Air Base

Group trailed by *Conqueror*

Burdwood Bank (shallow water)

Isla de los Estados

A R G E N T I N A

N

0   100 miles
0   200 km

on 25 April. By then, however, the prospect of a peaceful settlement was becoming increasingly remote. A week earlier three ships

British bombs explode near Stanley airport. The focal point of British attention was the runway. First attacked by a Vulcan bomber on 1 May, the runway had several hundred tons of ordnance devoted to it, including a Sea Slug missile. Because British maps were 1,000 m out, not enough high explosive landed on the runway to put it out of action for more than a short time. (Gamma)

comprising the destroyers *Plymouth* and *Antrim* and the tanker *Tidespring*, had pulled away from the main task force and sped to South Georgia. After reconnaissance by submarine and long-range aircraft showed no Argentine ships in the area, a team from D Squadron 22 SAS landed from *Antrim* on Fortuna Glacier near Leith on 21 April. This operation turned into a near disaster when the weather closed in, and two helicopters crashed on the glacier

before a third eventually extracted them. On the morning of 25 April the Argentine submarine *Santa Fe*, sent to reinforce the garrison, arrived at Grytviken, where it was attacked and crippled by helicopters from the British ships. Knowing that they had already been detected by long-range reconnaissance aircraft, the British decided on a direct assault on Grytviken by a scratch force of 75 Royal Marines, SAS and SBS from helicopters,

backed by fire from *Antrim* and *Plymouth*. The Argentine garrison surrendered shortly before dusk, followed by the surrender of the Leith garrison next day; in total 137 prisoners in a virtually bloodless victory. In London crowds gathered outside 10 Downing Street and sang 'Rule Britannia', while in New York an embarrassed and humiliated Costa Mendez rejected Haig's peace plan.

The failure of Haig's diplomatic offensive cleared the way for Peru, one of Argentina's supporters, to launch its own peace initiative, though the main task force was almost within striking distance of the Falklands. On 28 April, the day Britain announced that a total exclusion zone of 200 nautical miles around the Falklands would come into effect as of 1100 30 April, the Argentine navy put to sea. The following day (29 April) it split into two groups, one centred on the carrier moving north-west of the islands, and the other on *General Belgrano*, moving to the south of the Falklands. The British now faced a variety of threats coming from different directions – Aermaachis, Pucaras and Mentors from the Falkland airbases, high-performance jets from Argentine bases, two naval task forces, one capable of launching long-range air strikes, the other Exocets, and at least three submarines.

In the early hours of 1 May the British began the systematic reduction of the threats. An RAF Vulcan bomber, refuelled in flight from Ascension by 15 Victor tankers on an 8,000-mile round trip, dropped a stick of 21 1,000-pound bombs across Port Stanley airfield. Unknown to the RAF, the Argentine engineers who had constructed the airfield had made a mistake when plotting its position on survey maps. As a consequence, the airfield's position on maps the crew was using was 1,000 m from its actual position. Despite this disadvantage, one bomb hit the centre of the runway, cratering it badly and ensuring it could not be used by fast jets. As dawn broke, nine Harriers from *Hermes* dived down on Stanley airfield, attacking anti-aircraft positions and dropping cluster bombs amongst parked aircraft. Simultaneously, another four Harriers hit Darwin–Goose Green, destroying two

Hit by two torpedoes near her stern, the *General Belgrano* lists heavily. Commissioned as the USS *Phoenix* on 3 October 1938, she had survived the Japanese attack on Pearl Harbor on 7 December 1941, and saw creditable service throughout the Pacific War. The *Belgrano* was an old ship, and that allowed critics of the sinking to depict her as a museum piece, incapable of threatening the task force. In fact *Belgrano* was equipped with Exocets, and a salvo from her 12 6in guns could have sent any British warship to the bottom. (Rex Features)

Pucaras on the ground. Soon afterwards *Glamorgan*, *Alacrity* and *Arrow* steamed within gun range of the airfield and opened up, their total of four 4.5s pumping scores of shells into Argentine depots and positions.

Part of Woodward's plan was to provoke the Argentines into a reaction and it was not slow in coming. Sporadic encounters during the morning between Argentine and British air patrols were the prelude for an all-out Argentine attack in the afternoon. Several waves of aircraft – more than 40 in all – swept down on the British ships, now steaming eastwards at full speed. Rising to meet the attackers, Harriers fired their new Sidewinder AIM-9L air-to-air missiles and disposed of two Mirages, a Dagger and a Canberra. Shortly after dusk the British bombardment group put about, and by 2300 were once again lobbing shells on to where they thought the Argentines might have their defences. At about the same time the Argentine carrier force, cruising to the north-west of the Falklands, detected elements of the British task force to the south-east, at a range of about 300 miles. In the pre-dawn gloom of 2 May, the Argentines fuelled and armed their eight A-4 Skyhawks, but light winds prevented the launch of the heavily laden aircraft. The carrier group withdrew to the north, out of range of British reconnaissance, but still a potent threat to Woodward's task force.

South of the Falklands the nuclear submarine *Conqueror* had been shadowing the *Belgrano* task force as it zigzagged along the southern edge of the Burdwood Bank, an area of 1,000 square miles where the water was too shallow to allow the operation of a nuclear submarine. Already acutely aware of the danger posed by the carrier to the north west, Woodward also had to face the possibility that after dark the *General Belgrano* might suddenly steam north over the bank until she was within Exocet range of the Task Force. Ignoring the chain of command, he ordered *Conqueror* to attack the ship, an order which was relayed to and confirmed by the War Cabinet. Just before 1900, with the range now at 1,400 yards, *Conqueror* fired a spread of three Mark 8 torpedoes, two of which struck the *Belgrano* near her stern. She sank within 45 minutes, with the loss of 368 lives.

From 'Bomb Alley' to Mt Harriet

The news of the sinking of the *Belgrano* reverberated around the world like a shock wave. In the clashes thus far very few had died, and prisoners had been quickly returned via neutral nations to their homelands. All that now changed. The Junta rejected the peace plan put forward by Peru, which was much more favourable to Argentina than to Britain, and saved London the embarrassment of rejecting it unilaterally. There were to be other peace plans, but they were now more likely to fail than not because too many had died. Argentina claimed the ship had been outside the Total Exclusion Zone and was not posing a threat to the task force, an argument that was soon taken up by some Latin American and European nations, and elements of the British left. Britain did lose some support internationally, but the vast majority of the British people supported the sinking.

The international implications of the sinking did not worry Woodward. The event had sent the Argentine navy hurrying back to port, thus removing two of the threats that faced the task force. He now pressed home his advantage. During the next 24 hours Lynx helicopters sank and disabled two Argentine patrol boats on their way to the islands. An RAF Vulcan, too, paid another visit to Stanley, though thanks to the mapping error mentioned above the bombs missed the runway entirely. Shortly after 0800 on 4 May an Argentine Neptune patrol aircraft detected a radar emission from the task force. Less than three hours later two Super Etendard aircraft, scrambled from Rio Grande air base in Tierra del Fuego, loosed two Exocet missiles towards radar

The burnt-out hulk of HMS *Sheffield*. Hit by an Exocet on 2 May, *Sheffield* was soon ablaze. Twenty of her crew were killed and many more were injured, some with serious burns. The loss of the *Sheffield* induced task force commander Admiral Sandy Woodward to move his ships to the east, well out of range of aircraft based in Argentina. (Gamma)

blips only 12 miles distant. Two minutes later one of the missiles smashed into HMS *Sheffield*'s starboard side. The warhead failed to explode, but the momentum of the half-ton missile carried it into the bowels of the ship, where it disintegrated and poured out burning fuel. As fires spread throughout the ship *Yarmouth* and *Arrow* came alongside, paying out fire hoses and playing water on the hull. The battle to save *Sheffield* went on throughout the afternoon, but shortly before 1800 her commander, Captain Sam Salt, gave the order to abandon ship, and the burned-out hulk sank a week later, while under tow by *Yarmouth*. Of her 286 crew, 20 were dead and 24 injured, some with very severe burns.

The *Sheffield* was the first warship the Royal Navy had lost to enemy action since 1945. In London some of the younger members of the War Cabinet expressed misgivings, though they were soon steadied by those who had seen service in the Second World War. In the South Atlantic Woodward

LSVs cross-decking before the San Carlos landing. Despite the fact that weather conditions were worsening, HQ at Northwood insisted that troops on Canberra *transfer to landing craft while still at sea. The result was that 12 SAS troopers drowned when their helicopter lost power and plunged into the freezing Atlantic. (Department of War Studies, Sandhurst)*

put about and steamed eastwards until the task force was out of Exocet range, though its new position diminished the operational effectiveness of the Harrier. On 6 May he warned the amphibious force, still steaming south, that he would not be able to achieve aerial superiority before a landing. No longer willing to expose his carriers to the danger of Exocet attack, Woodward decided to provoke the Argentines into further attacks by sending his Type 22s and 42s in pairs close to the islands. The '42-22 combo', as it became known, was a missile trap, in which the Type 42's Sea Dart system would engage the Argentines at medium range, while the Type 22's Sea Wolf would deal with any aircraft at close range. The first success came on 9 May when *Coventry*, a Type 42, shot down two Skyhawks and a Puma helicopter. Three days later a combination of *Glasgow*, a Type 42, and *Brilliant*, a Type 22, shot down another three Skyhawks, while a fourth aircraft from a second attack wave was shot down by over-anxious Argentine gunners as it passed over Darwin–Goose Green. For the Argentine air force it was not a good day: a bomb from the second attack wave hit *Glasgow*, but passed through her without exploding.

The task force was winning the battle of attrition, but it was taking a long time. Mindful of the success of special force's operations against enemy airfields during the Second World War, on the night of 15 May the SAS landed on Pebble Island and destroyed six Pucaras, four Mentors and one Skyvan transport aircraft. The following night an eight-man SAS team landed in a Sea King outside Rio Grande airbase on Tierra del Fuego, but detecting an Argentine radar blip,

took off again and headed for Chile, where they set the helicopter on fire and handed themselves over to Chilean forces. This insertion was to have been the prelude for a full-scale raid, codenamed Operation Mikado, in which the SAS was to have crash-landed in two C-130 transports on Rio Grande airfield, destroyed the Super Etendards, and then escaped overland to Chilean territory. With the Argentines alerted, many at SAS HQ Hereford thought the attack was suicidal and it was cancelled, much to the annoyance of the SAS's director, Colonel Peter de la Billiere.

In addition to wearing down the Argentine air force the task force was sinking

Sidewinder AIM-L missiles. The Americans had emptied NATO stocks of the latest version of the Sidewinder, which a pilot could fire head on at an enemy aircraft, rather than having to manoeuvre behind it. The Sidewinder AIM-L gave British Harriers a considerable advantage over the Argentine Air Force. Of the 18 Argentine fixed wing aircraft shot down by Harriers, 17 fell victim to the AIM-L. (Gamma)

British Aerospace Rapier surface to air missile. The missile can fly at a speed in excess of Mach 2 and has an altitude of 10,000 ft. It is guided to the target either by line-of-sight radio command signals, or in darkness and poor visibility, by a tracker radar. Much hope was placed in the Rapier air defence system, but technical and logistic difficulties were to dog it throughout the campaign. The Rapier system succeeded in shooting down only three enemy aircraft. (Department of War Studies, Sandhurst)

Argentine ships sailing to and around the islands, testing Argentine defences, and landing SAS and SBS teams to gather intelligence. This up-to-date intelligence, combined with the detailed knowledge of the Falklands' coastline supplied by Ewan Southby-Tailyour, a Royal Marine officer who had sailed his own yacht around the islands in 1977, allowed the amphibious commanders to agree on a landing site, San Carlos Water, on the west coast of East Falkland. From the Royal Navy's viewpoint it was a sheltered anchorage, surrounded by hills that gave good cover from air attack, and was accessible from both north and south through Falkland Sound, avoiding the risk of a submarine bottling up the fleet. Woodward confirmed that Falkland Sound was not mined by the expedient of sailing *Alacrity* through it at night. The beaches were suitable for landing craft, well out of range of any Argentine artillery, and were only lightly defended. Once the beachhead was established, its surrounding hills would make it easy to defend. Its only drawback was its distance of 56 miles from Port Stanley, the main objective, but the amphibious group was well supplied with heavy-lift helicopters, which would allow a rapid advance on the capital.

On 19 May the task force rendezvoused with the Amphibious Group to the north of the Falklands. The War Cabinet, mindful of the impact the loss of *Canberra* with most of 3 Brigade aboard might have on international opinion, ordered a complex cross-decking operation from the liner into the *Fearless* and *Intrepid*. The sea was high, conditions were deteriorating, and a helicopter carrying members of 22 SAS lost power and plunged into the ocean, killing 12 troopers. An avoidable disaster at this stage made everyone feel depressed but morale remained high, although tinged with a sense of apprehension. Lest his men lose their edge, the commander of 3 Para, Lt Colonel Pike, had told them that it might be like Gallipoli, the disastrous landing on the Dardanelles on 25 April 1915. Others thought of Dieppe, Tarawa and Omaha

beach. D Day was set for shortly after midnight on 20/21 May, when the weather forecast promised poor visibility.

The first Argentines to encounter the British were a detachment of 20 at Fanning Head, an 800 ft bluff which dominated San Carlos. Well before dawn they ran into a patrol of SBS which had been dropped by helicopter to the east: nine Argentines were killed or surrendered, the remainder escaped in the dark. Another Argentine platoon ensconced on the high ground behind the San Carlos settlement made the first sighting of the task force. After reporting the landings the platoon withdrew hurriedly, shooting down two British Gazelle helicopters and killing three of the crew. Pucaras from Goose Green and an Aermacchi from Stanley soon arrived to attack the beachhead but ran into intense ground fire, two Pucaras going down in flames. From the surviving pilots' reports Menendez surmised that this was a subsidiary operation, designed to draw his forces westward and uncover the real objective, Port Stanley. In these circumstances the only major response could come from the Argentine Air Force: thus Menendez requested air strikes from the mainland.

As the amphibious task force sailed into San Carlos Water the British commanders were painfully aware of their vulnerability to air attack. Sea Harrier pilots and some of the escort captains had urged Woodward to establish a layered defence consisting of Sea Harrier interception patrols well out to the west of West Falkland, a patrol line of destroyers and frigates further east (but still to the west of West Falkland), and finally the guns and missiles of the escorts in Falkland Sound and San Carlos Water, supplemented by Rapiers, which would be set up immediately the landing had taken place. Woodward was strongly opposed to the idea of a layered defence. He believed it would expose the warships patrolling off West Falkland to unnecessary risks, and the Sea Harrier patrols could only be maintained if the carriers of the task force moved well to the west, thus endangering his most

Troops and supplies land at San Carlos. The landing operation did not go smoothly, and some of the landing craft grounded on sand bars some distance from the shore. Fortunately Argentine opposition was slight and quickly overcome. (Department of War Studies, Sandhurst)

important warships. Woodward insisted on the adoption of an alternative air defence plan, the creation of a defensive box of warships around the amphibious force. A mixture of missiles and gunfire would shoot down anything flying into the box. To minimise confusion, Harriers were forbidden to fly into the box themselves or to attack Argentine aircraft once they had flown into it. The hills around San Carlos Water would protect the amphibious group from Exocet attack. Unfortunately they would also make it difficult for the ships' radar to pick up attacking aircraft before they were literally on top of them.

The first Argentine jets screamed down on San Carlos at 1030, and they kept coming until 1530. Of the 45 aircraft dispatched (26 Skyhawks and 19 Daggers), 26 managed to carry out attacks on British ships. Argentine pilots, probably conscious of the political impact of such sinkings, concentrated their attentions on the British warships. In order to avoid British missiles,

Argentine pilots came in very low. This allowed the Argentines to achieve an extraordinary degree of accuracy, but it also meant that at least 10 of their bombs did not have time to fuse and failed to detonate on impact. Of the five warships hit, only *Ardent* was sinking. *Brilliant* and *Broadsword* had been damaged by cannon fire, and *Argonaut* and *Antrim* had been temporarily put out of action with unexploded bombs inside them. Ten Argentine aircraft, five Daggers and five Skyhawks, had been shot down, all but one of them by Sea Harriers.

The attrition rate had been high but the Argentines had badly mauled the Amphibious Group's escorts. Unfortunately for the Argentines, bad weather over southern Argentina on 22 May prevented flying until very late in the day, when two ineffectual strikes were made. On 23 and 24 May the Argentine Air Force was back; a total of 33 sorties reached San Carlos and hit another four warships. As on 21 May, the Argentines again came in very low: this time not a single bomb detonated. On the evening of 22 May, however, a bomb lodged in *Antelope* blew up while engineers were attempting to defuse it. The intensity of the attacks on 21, 23 and 24 May led Woodward to experiment with forward deployment by sending *Coventry* and

The Landings 21 May 1982

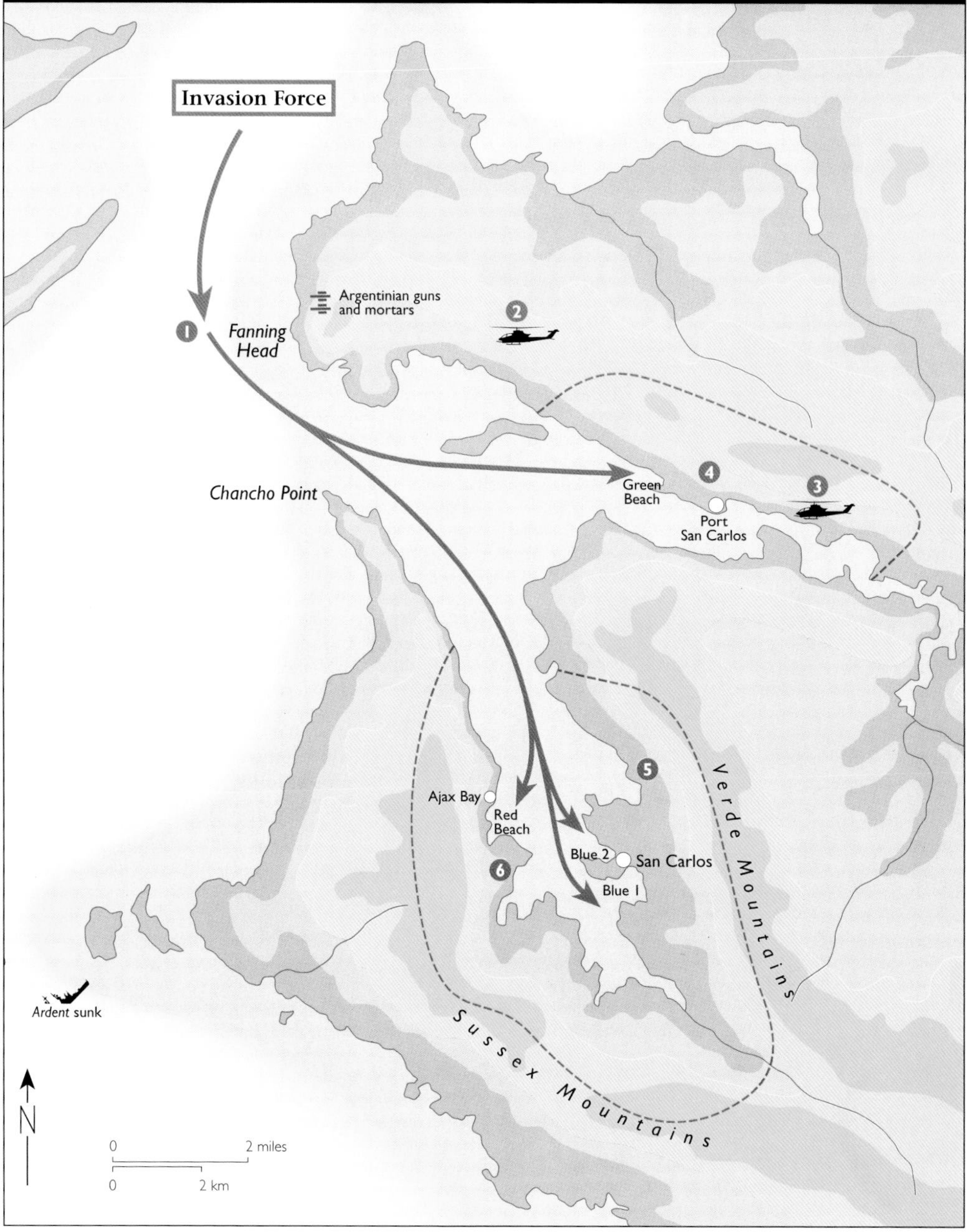

Invasion Force

Argentinian guns
and mortars

① Fanning
Head

Chancho Point

Green
Beach

④

③

Port
San Carlos

⑤

Verde Mountains

Ajax Bay
Red
Beach

⑥

Blue 2 ○ San Carlos

Blue 1

Ardent sunk

Sussex Mountains

N

0 — 2 miles

0 — 2 km

1. Paras and Marines transfer to landing craft
2. SBS land from helicopter and attack Argentine forces on Fanning Head
3. Argentine platoon retreating from Port San Carlos shoots down two Gazelle helicopters
4. Landing of 3 Para and 42 Commando
5. Landing of 40 Commando and 3 Brigade HQ
6. Landing of 2 Para and 45 Commando. 2 Para subsequently moves up to Sussex Mountains

Broadsword westward to form an early warning line off Pebble Island. On 25 May they were soon spotted by Argentine observation posts who vectored air attacks on to them. *Broadsword* was hit by a bomb, which once again failed to explode, but *Coventry* was less fortunate, suffering three direct hits which killed 19 of the crew and sank her. Meanwhile in late afternoon two Super Etendards, their range increased by refuelling from a KC-130 tanker, picked up a large blip to the north-east on their radar. Believing they had located *Hermes* the Argentines loosed their Exocets and hit *Atlantic Conveyor*, a 28,000-ton container ship loaded with supplies and three Chinook and six Wessex heavy-lift helicopters. Fires spread throughout the ship, detonating cluster bombs, and killing 12 of the crew, including her master, Captain Ian North. The smoking hulk drifted for several days before she foundered.

By the evening of 25 May, British commanders were becoming increasingly worried. In the previous four days Argentine air attacks had sunk or damaged eight warships and transports, losses of an intensity not experienced since the evacuation of Crete in June 1941. But the attacks of 25 May proved to be the high water mark of Argentina's air campaign. Further raids were made against the actual beachhead on 27 and 29 May. These caused casualties and inflicted some degree of damage, but nothing like the incessant attacks of 21, 23 and 24 May was seen again. Argentina, quite simply, was running out of aircraft and pilots. As early as 23 May casualties had caused the withdrawal from action of the highly skilled 3rd Naval Fighter and Attack Squadron. By 29 May some 90 sorties had reached the operational area of which 21 had been shot down, 12 by Sea Harriers. By a process of slow attrition the British were establishing a degree of air superiority over the islands.

While the air battle raged, 3 Commando Brigade was busy establishing a beachhead. An amphibious operation of this sort, without a proper rehearsal, enough purpose-built ships or air superiority, violated many of the lessons that had been painfully learned during the Second World War. But in the event the landing went relatively smoothly. A navigational error caused some delay but the landing craft were guided in by SBS men who had infiltrated San Carlos a week earlier, and 3,000 men came ashore with very few accidents. Getting equipment

and supplies ashore proved rather more difficult. Owing to the speed at which the ships of the task force had sailed from Britain there had been no time to store equipment tactically. The wait at Ascension Island had given 3 Commando Brigade's logisticians a chance to sort out the confusion, but when the task force sailed south again much still remained to be done. Thompson and Clapp decided to keep some of the supplies afloat, in part to give the logisticians the time and space to continue sorting, in part because the only place in San Carlos suitable for a logistic base was a small area around Ajax Bay. Here a disused mutton factory could provide some cover, but it would rapidly become congested. The first Argentine air attacks wrecked the entire plan. As much as possible had to be disembarked and big ships such as *Canberra* and *Norland* had to be returned to the protection of the task force as quickly as possible. Men worked frenetically, but when *Canberra* and *Norland* steamed away, they took with them the unit stores of two commandos and both parachute battalions, items which ranged from vital replacement battle batteries to first line stocks of ammunition not carried on the men, such as mortar, Milan and Wombat anti-tank rounds, and a complete resupply of small-arms ammunition. Also on board the *Canberra* were 90,000 rations, enough to feed the brigade for 18 days.

On 23 May Thompson had received orders to proceed with the investment of Port Stanley. To this end, on the following night the SBS landed at Port Salvador on the north coast of East Falkland to reconnoitre the area of Teal Inlet, so that it could be used as a forward logistic base to support operations against Stanley. On the same night helicopters took the reconnaissance elements of D Squadron 22 SAS to Mt Kent, from where Stanley was clearly visible to the east. This was a preliminary move to the establishment of a strong position near Stanley by moving troops by helicopter across the island. The following evening Thompson's plans lay in ruins, because the loss of the *Atlantic Conveyor* removed at one stroke virtually all his transport machines.

Given the critical nature of his situation Thompson would have preferred to wait for additional helicopters coming south with 5 Infantry Brigade. But the War Cabinet and Northwood were facing mounting political pressure. Ever since the British landing the Security Council had been debating in open session. On 26 May Ireland tabled a resolution for an immediate cease-fire. Although this was watered down to a request that the Secretary General undertake a new peace mission, diplomatically the situation seemed to be moving in Argentina's favour. Britain might eventually be forced to use her veto, leaving her diplomatically isolated and exposed as an opponent of peace. Meanwhile, backbench pressure mounted against the government. Questions were being asked in the Commons about the landing force's apparent lack of progress. The Marines and Paras had come ashore on 21 May, British ships were being sunk, but the landing force seemed to be content to sit in the beachhead. Older MPs who had lived through the Second World War reinforced the point by invoking memories of the Germans bottling up the beachheads at Anzio and Normandy in 1944.

Pressure for immediate action was also building up from within 3 Commando Brigade. The paratroop battalions had come ashore eager and ready for immediate action. Instead they found themselves being ordered to dig in on the hillsides. There they waited, cold and wet, and subject to air attacks. The spirits of 2 Para improved on 23 May when

their commander, Lieutenant Colonel 'H' Jones, received orders to prepare a raid on Darwin–Goose Green to eliminate the Pucara threat. Lack of helicopters ruled out a move by air and navigational difficulties ruled out a move by sea. Much to the annoyance of the paratroopers, on 24 May Thompson, who had always regarded the raid as a diversion from the main effort, ordered its cancellation.

In London the War Cabinet was not ignorant of Thompson's logistic problems, but was increasingly concerned to maintain the momentum, even if this meant running serious risks. Acting on the government's instructions, on 26 May, the day after the loss of the *Atlantic Conveyor*, HQ Northwood gave Thompson direct and explicit instructions to undertake two major operations simultaneously: he was to send 2 Para to raid Darwin–Goose Green and an even more substantial force to invest Port Stanley. That night 2 Para moved off Sussex Mountain towards Camilla Creek House and Darwin–Goose Green, while soon after dawn 45 Commando, followed shortly after by 3 Para, set off for Douglas and Teal Inlet settlements respectively. All the columns were heavily laden, and were expected to march long distances over difficult terrain in high winds and low temperatures. Their logistic support, at least initially, depended on what they could carry supplemented by whatever the helicopters could land as soon as they became available. Operations of this sort could not have been contemplated, let alone undertaken, with troops less well trained and less highly motivated than the paratroopers and Royal Marines.

Reaching Camilla Creek before dawn on 27 May, Jones sent two reconnaissance patrols towards suspected Argentine

Lieutenant Colonel 'H' Jones. A newcomer to the Parachute Regiment, 'H' Jones earned a reputation as a fire-eater. In exercises he was almost always declared 'dead'. His plans for the battle were subsequently criticised as too restrictive by those who had walked the ground and had years to think about how it should be fought. Jones had only a few hours. (Department of War Studies, Sandhurst)

positions. Jones had only been with the battalion a short time but he had already developed a reputation as an aggressive 'fire-eater'. In exercises he always led from the front, so much so that umpires usually declared him 'dead'. On the basis of reports from earlier SAS patrols, Jones believed that the settlement was defended by at most 500 Argentines, which would be easy meat for his Paras. As the morning wore on, however, his patrols reported back very heavy Argentine movements, the first intimation that the SAS had been wrong. In fact, the settlements held 1,500; with added reinforcements the number was to rise to 1,630. In addition the settlements were in an ideal defensive position, on a five-mile-long isthmus that was only about 2,000 yards wide. The Argentine front was covered by a mine field, behind which they had positioned in successive defence lines 11 medium machine-guns, three 105mm guns, and three 35mm anti-aircraft guns.

Shortly before 1130 as the morning mist cleared, the Argentines spotted one of the patrols and opened up with heavy machine guns. A Harrier strike, delayed by the mist, eventually allowed the patrols to withdraw,

but Argentine anti-aircraft guns shot the tail off one of the aircraft, forcing the pilot to eject. At about this time Jones's HQ tuned into the BBC and received a dreadful shock. The announcer stated that 'a parachute battalion is poised and ready to assault Darwin–Goose Green'. The BBC's Robert Fox, who was attached to 2 Para, recalled that Jones exploded into anger: 'I'll sue John Nott – I'll sue the MoD –I'll sue Thatcher!' Jones knew that there was now no prospect of surprise. There was also little prospect of adequate fire support. His second-in-command, Major Chris Keeble, suggested delay, but Jones would have none of it. He was 42 years old, he was commanding his own battalion, and he knew that this chance was unlikely to come again. 'Chris, I've waited 22 years for this,' he said, 'I'm not going to wait any longer.'

Jones knew that his only real chance was to attack at night, but that this would

Argentine prisoners lie on the ground at the ruins of Boca House. The fall of the Boca House position cleared the left flank of the Argentine defences, and allowed B and D companies to work their way around enemy trenches on the reverse slope of the Darwin Hill position. (Department of War Studies, Sandhurst)

Battle of Darwin–Goose Green

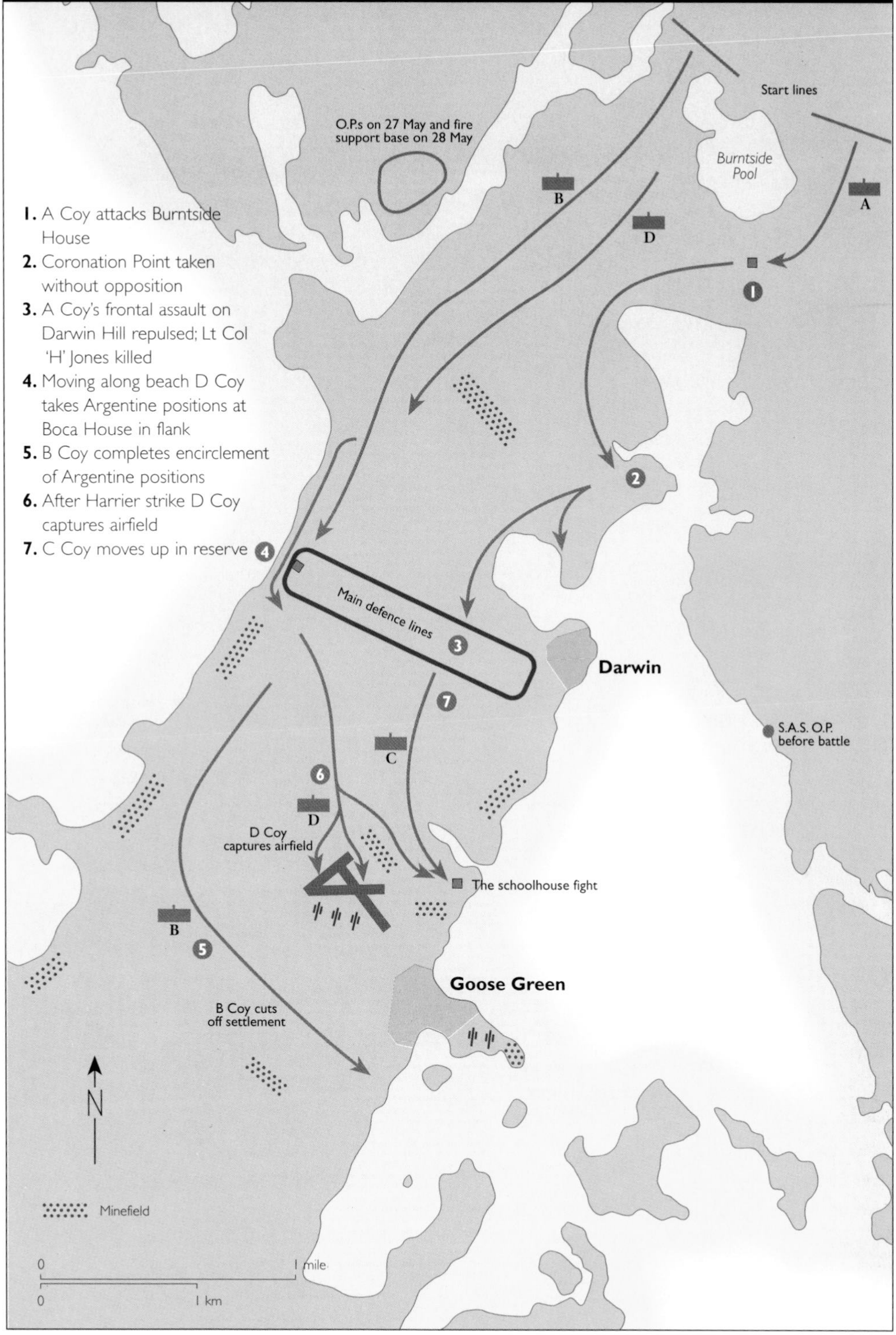

Start lines

O.P.s on 27 May and fire
support base on 28 May

Burntside
Pool

B

A

D

❶

1. A Coy attacks Burntside
   House
2. Coronation Point taken
   without opposition
3. A Coy's frontal assault on
   Darwin Hill repulsed; Lt Col
   'H' Jones killed
4. Moving along beach D Coy
   takes Argentine positions at
   Boca House in flank
5. B Coy completes encirclement
   of Argentine positions
6. After Harrier strike D Coy
   captures airfield
7. C Coy moves up in reserve **❹**

❷

Main defence lines **❸**

Darwin

❼

C

● S.A.S. O.P.
before battle

❻

D

D Coy
captures airfield

B

The schoolhouse fight

B

❺

Goose Green

B Coy cuts
off settlement

N

⬛ Minefield

0 ———————————— 1 mile

0 ———————————— 1 km

Argentine surrender at Darwin–Goose Green. The British were astonished when long columns of Argentines emerged to surrender. Prisoners outnumbered captors by about 3:1. (Department of War Studies, Sandhurst)

impose immense problems on command and control. All commanders fear that fighting in the dark will result in friendly fire casualties, the so called 'blue on blue'. Jones determined to overcome this by devising a rigid battle plan with six distinct phases, all of them carefully timetabled. The first two phases involved securing the start line. The attack began at 0230 in pouring rain, with A Company on the left flank advancing towards Darwin Hill, and B and D Companies on the right moving towards Boca House, an isolated settlement. By 0400 the initial objectives had been reached and A Company was now pulling ahead of B and D Companies. A Company commander, Captain Farrar-Hockley, radioed Jones for permission to

attack the next objective, Darwin Hill, but the colonel was worried that a further advance by A Company would unbalance the attack. In order to get a clearer idea of the situation Jones went forward with his protection party, reaching Farrer-Hockley's position just as dawn was breaking. When he saw Darwin Hill loom through the morning gloom, he must have realised that the delay he had imposed had been a mistake. He immediately ordered a frontal assault up Darwin Hill.

As the Paras moved forward, the Argentines opened up with everything they had. Charging up a steep slope, the Para attack was soon canalised by a gully full of gorse, into which the Argentines poured a withering fire. Within seconds the men of the leading platoon were dead, wounded, or had gone to ground. Realising that he would have to get around the Argentine positions, Jones took his protection party and charged up a re-entrant to the right of the Hill. He almost made it. As he single-handedly stormed an Argentine trench from the rear, he was cut down by a burst of machine gun fire from behind. The first part of the battle had gone badly and Jones had died courageously, trying to put things right. He was to be awarded a posthumous VC.

The situation was desperate and the Paras responded with the grim – some say sick – humour of the British army. An A Company radio operator, pinned in the gorse gully by an almost solid stream of fire, was calling into his mike 'Kirk to Enterprise, Kirk to Enterprise, for God's sake Scotty, beam me up!' A few yards away a corporal, his leg severed by a burst of machine gun fire, lay on the ground shouting 'I've lost my leg – I've lost my leg.' In the soon to be immortal reply, a young Para lying just behind him shouted back reassuringly, 'No you haven't corp – its back here next to me.' About 1,000 yards to the west B Company, too, was pinned down by heavy machine guns supplemented by direct fire from anti-aircraft guns. Because movement was for the moment impossible the Paras decided not to waste time, but instead cooked and ate breakfast while shells and bullets screamed a few feet overhead. Crawling up to the position Robert Fox found the scene almost surreal – the Paras were joking and chatting as though they were on a picnic, not in the middle of a battle.

Major Chris Keeble was now in command. As he went forward 2 Para's RSM called him back. He looked Keeble in the eye and said, 'You, sir, are going to do fucking well!' Keeble recalled that as he made his way forward he felt like a million dollars. A Company was clearly in a mess. Keeble therefore concentrated on the right flank. B Company managed to pull back from exposed positions on the left of Darwin Hill, and worked south to attack Boca House, which they bombarded with Milan wire-guided anti-tank missiles. Further west, Major Phil Neame pulled D Company down a low cliff on to a narrow beach. Protected by the cliff from Argentine fire Neame now led his Paras in single file along the narrow beach, until they could attack the Boca House positions in the flank. At about 1400 B and D Companies managed to push south again, taking a few yards at a time. To their left, A Company was pulverising Argentine positions on Darwin Hill with Karl Gustav anti-tank rockets, and then attacking the shaken defenders with grenades and bayonets. Argentine aircraft, Aermacchis and Pucaras, swept down, straffing with rockets and cannon. The Paras fired back with machine guns and Blowpipe missiles, downing an Aermacchi. Soon a Pucara, armed with napalm, was down as well, crashing near some Paras. The liquid sprayed from ruptured tanks, drenching everyone, but mercifully did not ignite. By 1500 B Company had reached the north-western edge of the airfield, where it was again pinned down by intense direct fire from the Argentine's 35 mm anti-aircraft guns. At 1535 two Harriers arrived, dropped cluster bombs on the Argentine positions, and B Company, supported on its left flank by D Company, pushed to the middle of the airfield, C Company moving up in reserve. By dusk the Paras were only 400 yards from Goose Green; by now Argentine 105mms were firing with their barrels vertical.

The night of 28/29 May seemed interminable, both for Keeble and for the Argentine ground-force commander, Lieutenant Colonel Piaggi. The Paras had now been awake for about 40 hours and had been fighting for about 14 hours. They had exhausted their own ammunition hours earlier, and had kept the battle going by using captured Argentine ordnance. Some, indeed, had abandoned their own sub-machine guns and Self-Loading-Rifles (SLRs) for the Argentine FN30, which could be converted to fully automatic by the flick of a lever. The Argentines were also exhausted. Despite their overwhelming numerical superiority, they had been forced back steadily throughout the day. That night most Paras thought they had lost the battle, but decided to carry on as though they hadn't. The Argentines also thought they had lost the battle and decided the sensible thing to do was surrender. The British had suffered 17 dead and 33 wounded, the Argentines 55 dead and 86 wounded. In addition, 1,536 physically uninjured Argentines became prisoners of war.

The battle of Darwin–Goose Green defied the logic of force ratios. The British never achieved more than parity at the point of attack and overall were heavily outnumbered by the Argentines, who were well dug in, equipped with automatic weapons, supplied with large quantities of ammunition, and

supported by mortar and artillery fire and ground attack aircraft. Moreover, the attacking British, at the end of a long supply line, frequently ran short of ammunition, and were able to maintain the attack only by re-equipping themselves from Argentine positions as they overran them. The

Islanders reported that in the last stages of the occupation terrified Argentine troops believed that the British were not taking prisoners. In fact, once they became prisoners many troops received the first warm food and medical attention they had had in days. (Gamma)

surrendering Argentines could not at first believe they had been defeated by a force less than one-third the size of their own. Piaggi was particularly mortified because he had reported to Stanley at one stage that he was being attacked by the entire British brigade.

The logic of war dictated that the paratroopers should not have won, but they did. The victory depended on unquantifiable factors – leadership, training, morale, esprit de corps, and fighting spirit. In Britain news

The Yomp/Tab. The Royal Marines Yomp and the Paras Tab. Whatever the name, the march of the heavily laden Marines and Paras across East Falkland was an epic of endurance. The most highly trained infantry in the world at that time, the loss of the helicopters was not going to immobilise the Marines and Paras while they still had their legs. (MOD, print from MARS)

of the battle led to a massive upsurge in parliamentary and national morale: the last time Britain had celebrated a crushing victory was in 1945. Elsewhere the news was greeted with disbelief and then, as the facts became irrefutable, with incredulity. Britain's international prestige rose steadily. The battle had a profound effect on the conduct of the campaign. The gloom and despondency that gripped Menendez and his headquarters soon infected many Argentine officers, though most conscripts remained unaware of the scale of the defeat. Two Para's attack also served to confirm Menendez's preconception that the drive on Stanley would come from the south, probably along the axis of the Fitzroy–Stanley track. On 29 May he ordered 4th Infantry regiment to occupy Two Sisters and Mt Harriet, which would cover an advance from the south-west.

During the battle for Darwin–Goose Green, the Argentines had moved reserve forces positioned in the Mt Kent area to reinforce Piaggi's increasingly beleaguered soldiers. Unknown to the Argentines, this move allowed 22 SAS, which had been infiltrating on to Mt Kent since the night of 24/25 May, to secure much of the area without a fight. By 29 May, when the Argentines finally discovered that the British had seized a mountain that commanded splendid views of their positions to the west of Stanley, the British were firmly established. That night two large Argentine special force patrols attempted to recapture the mountain. Ambushed by the SAS, the Argentines fought all night, losing two dead and six captured. The following night the Tactical HQ of 42 Commando with K Company, the Mortar Troop, and three light guns flew to reinforce the SAS. A search through abandoned Argentine positions on the mountain yielded an invaluable prize; a map that showed the location of every Argentine unit and the boundaries within which it was expected to operate. It was clear from the dispositions that Argentine attention was fixed on the southern axis.

In the meantime 45 Commando and 3 Para had been marching towards Teal Inlet. The leading elements of 45 Commando reached Douglas settlement at about 1300 on 28 May while 3 Para arrived at Teal Inlet at 2300 the same evening. Early the following morning they were joined by a troop of light tanks from the Blues and Royals. The move secured the shoreline of Port Salvador which at one point, Estancia Bay, lay only 15 miles north-west of Stanley. On 30 May, however, two Argentine UH-I Iroquois helicopters deposited a patrol of 16 men at Top Malo House which sat athwart the main line of communication between Teal Inlet and Estancia Bay, from where they would have a good view of British operations. It was a daring move but it had been spotted by a British observation post. Soon after dawn on 31 May 19 men of the Royal Marines Mountain and Arctic Warfare cadre landed by helicopter in a valley out of sight of Top Malo House and moved stealthily on the Argentine position. A fierce firefight ensued, in which every member of the Argentine patrol was killed or captured.

On the night of 31 May/1June an LCU conducted an improvised sweep of the main channel through Port Salvador. The following night Sir Percivale made the first logistic run from San Carlos, bringing with it a Royal Corps of Transport Mexeflote to land supplies at Teal Inlet. A round trip from Teal to 3 Para's positions was about 15 miles, as opposed to 100 miles from San Carlos. The whole business of supply was speeded up, but life for the troops investing Stanley remained unpleasant. Vincent Bramley, a 3 Para Lance Corporal, recalled that

within two weeks we looked like a rag and bone army. Our faces were drawn with the loss of weight, our uniforms matted and soaked, we were hungry for solid food, and our boots, badly and cheaply made, were falling to pieces.

The men tried to dig weapons' pits into the peat, and found that very soon they were half full of water. At night the temperature fell to below freezing, there were frequent snow squalls, and the wind never seemed to drop below about 15 knots. Once men became wet they stayed wet. There was water aplenty, but all of it was heavily polluted with peat. The men drank it nevertheless – there was nothing else – and the result was that virtually everyone suffered from chronic diarrhoea, to the extent that most cut the seat out of their trousers. Trench foot, a condition associated with the wetter parts of the Western Front during the First World War, soon became widespread.

On 30 May Major General Jeremy Moore and his staff had arrived at San Carlos. Moore approved Thompson's existing plans and Thompson, reverting to the command of 3 Commando Brigade, removed himself and his HQ to Teal Inlet the following day. Pressure on Moore to bring operations to a speedy conclusion was now intense. On 31 May President Reagan phoned Mrs Thatcher to voice his worries over the tide of hostile opinion that seemed to be sweeping Latin America, an indication that American support was becoming less steadfast. In New York, Britain's ambassador to the United Nations, Sir Antony Parsons, was facing yet another ceasefire resolution, this time from

Panama and Spain. Parsons managed to delay the vote in the Security Council until 4 June, when the resolution was supported by nine countries, including China and the USSR, with four abstaining. Britain was forced to use her veto, and was supported by the United States. Almost immediately, however, Jeanne Kirkpatrick, the US ambassador to the UN, announced that were it possible to do so, she would change the American vote from a no to an abstention.

With Britain's international strategy apparently in the process of unravelling, Moore rushed ahead with the deployment of 5 Infantry Brigade, which had arrived in San Carlos on 2 June after cross-decking from the *QE2* in Cumberland Sound on the coast of South Georgia. Moore had travelled south aboard the *QE2* with 5 Infantry Brigade's commander, Brigadier Tony Wilson: during this time it was agreed that 5 Infantry Brigade would join in the attack on Stanley

5 Brigade landing at San Carlos water. Congestion at the beachhead was to some extent unavoidable, but it also suggests that the soldiers of 5 Brigade had yet to experience an air attack. (Department of War Studies, Sandhurst)

by coming from the south. Moore intended initially to move 5 Infantry Brigade by helicopter to Goose Green, a first step to opening up the southern axis of advance via the settlement of Fitzroy. However, 5 Infantry Brigade had set sail with painfully inadequate logistic assets. They would only be able to move with the aid of logistic support removed from 3 Commando Brigade. Virtually all the task force's helicopters were committed to the build-up and sustainment of 3 Commando Brigade in the Mt Kent area.

Some helicopters were made available on 2 June to airlift the 1/7th to join 2 Para at Goose Green. The rest of the brigade would have to march. The Welsh Guards set out on 3 June but after 50 minutes their officers, realising their men were already exhausted, called a halt and returned to San Carlos. In the meantime a patrol from 2 Para had flown in a Scout helicopter 20 miles due east of Goose Green to Sun Inlet House, from where they had telephoned Fitzroy, and learned from the islanders that the small Argentine garrison had withdrawn. On hearing this news Major Chris Keeble immediately commandeered the Chinook that had been seconded for logistic work to 5 Infantry Brigade for the day, and airlifted two companies and the headquarters of 2 Para to Fitzroy. This move, implemented without the knowledge of Moore's headquarters, posed severe problems. Although some Sea King helicopters were detailed to lift the rest of 2 Para to Fitzroy settlement and nearby Bluff Cove, there was no means immediately available of sustaining, let alone reinforcing, 2 Para, who were left with little ammunition and no air cover in an advanced position overlooked by an Argentine observation post.

With helicopters at a premium, the only way for Wilson to move the bulk of the brigade was by sea. The large amphibious ships Fearless and Intrepid could easily have carried out the move in a single lift, but the navy was reluctant to risk these ships so close to Stanley. As a consequence, on the night of 5/6 June, Intrepid carried only one of

5 Infantry Brigade's battalions, the 2nd Scots Guards, and then only as far as Lively Point, about halfway between San Carlos and Fitzroy. Here the Scots Guards transferred to Intrepid's four landing craft under the command of Major Ewan Southby-Tailyour for the remainder of the voyage, while Intrepid put about for the comparative safety of San Carlos. At first sea conditions were relatively good, with poor visibility. But the weather deteriorated as the landing craft rounded Lively Point. The frigate HMS Cardiff, returning from bombarding Stanley, sighted the landing craft. She had not been informed of friendly movements in the area and thus fired a star shell to illuminate the craft before attacking. A rapid exchange of terse signals by Aldiss Lamp only narrowly averted what might have been a serious friendly-fire incident.

Back in San Carlos, the following afternoon the Welsh Guards embarked in HMS Fearless. Commodore Clapp, Brigadier Wilson and Major Southby-Tailyour, who had flown by helicopter back from Bluff Cove, had together formulated a plan. Fearless was to carry only two landing craft, leaving two at San Carlos for logistic offloading. Off Lively Point, Fearless was to rendezvous with Southby-Tailyour's four landing craft, which would sail from Bluff Cove to meet her. But when Southby-Tailyour flew back to Bluff Cove he discovered three of his landing craft were missing: not until the following morning did he learn that 2 Para had commandeered them to move supplies to Fitzroy. When Fearless reached the rendezvous point at 0200 on 7 June and could not find Southby-Tailyour's landing craft, her captain had no alternative but to launch the two landing craft he was carrying, and to return to San Carlos with the remainder of the Welsh Guards.

On the afternoon of 7 June the remainder of the Welsh Guards embarked on Sir Galahad and she sailed that night, arriving at Fitzroy at 0800 on the following morning. The officers in charge were under the impression that they should have been landed further east at Bluff Cove, where the

Closing the net

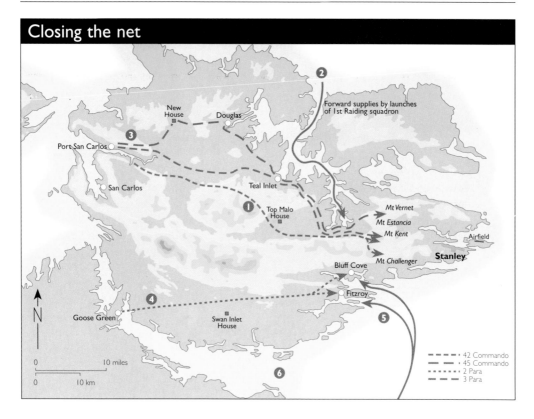

1. SAS followed by 42 Commando move by helicopter to Mt Kent 25–30 May.
2. SBS reconnoitre Teal Inlet 25 May. HQ 3 Brigade moves in 1 June.
3. 3 Para and 45 Commando 'tab' and 'yomp' across the island 27–30 May.
4. 2 Para by helicopter 3 June.
5. 2 Scots Guards and 1 Welsh Guards move to Fitzroy and Bluff Cove by sea 6–8 June.
6. Argentine Skyhawks bomb *Sir Galahad* and *Sir Tristram* 8 June.

rest of the battalion had bivouacked, and refused to disembark. They were reluctant to be separated from their heavy equipment, and they could see no point in subjecting their men to a tiring overland march when *Sir Galahad* was due to sail to Bluff Cove later in the day. Major Southby-Tailyour urged them to come ashore at any event and wait on the beach while unloading was under way: but they again refused because the only landing craft available were already loaded with ammunition. Early in the afternoon an unloaded landing craft became free: it was on the point of embarking the Welsh Guards

when it was commandeered by a Lieutenant Colonel of the RAMC to move his ambulance teams ashore.

During the five hours *Sir Galahad* had been at anchor, an Argentine observation post 10 miles away on Mt Harriet had radioed details of this and other British shipping movements (*Sir Tristram* was also unloading supplies in Fitzroy) via Stanley to mainland Argentine air force units. Mainland air bases scrambled eight Skyhawks and six Daggers, of which five Skyhawks and five Daggers reached the islands. Flying up Falkland Sound before turning to attack Fitzroy from the west, the Daggers spotted and bombed HMS *Plymouth*, scoring four direct hits, none of which detonated. Two Sea Harriers on routine patrol south of Fitzroy turned north-west in pursuit of the Daggers. Meanwhile the Skyhawks flew on to Fitzroy. The British had already set up four Rapier missile launchers, but the launcher covering the harbour had been damaged in transit and was out of action while a new sighting mechanism was being fitted. The

Skyhawks hit *Sir Tristram* with two bombs, one passing straight through the ship without detonating, the other exploding on the vehicle deck and killing two crewmen. The attack on *Sir Galahad* was launched from a higher altitude than usual. Three bombs crashed into the ship, their casings burst open, and the explosive contents burnt fiercely, creating fireballs. For the British this was the single bloodiest incident of the war: 46 men died on *Sir Galahad* and another 150 were injured, some very seriously. Two hours later the Argentines were back. Four Skyhawks, attempting to attack Bluff Cove, were driven off by intense ground fire from the Scots Guards, who discharged 18,500 rounds in just 45 seconds. Swinging around on Fitzroy, the Skyhawks encountered a barrage of at least seven Rapier missiles, and broke off the attack. Yet another flight of four Skyhawks spotted the landing craft *Foxtrot Four* halfway between Goose Green and Fitzroy and launched a devastating attack, killing six of the crew. The landing craft was saved from almost certain destruction by the arrival of two Sea Harriers, which promptly shot down three of the Skyhawks with Sidewinders.

Meanwhile on the northern side of East Falkland, 3 Commando Brigade's build-up was continuing unabated. Patrols from

Sir Galahad at Bluff Cove, 8 June 1982. With nearly 200 casualties the attack on *Sir Galahad* was the single most costly incident of the war for the British. An accretion of errors combined with plain bad luck to leave the ship exposed to Argentine attack for more than four hours. (Rex Features)

3 Para and 45 and 42 Commando had pushed into the hills and mountains ringing Stanley to the west and had largely confirmed the dispositions outlined in the Argentine map captured on Mt Kent. By the evening of 6 June Thompson believed he had enough information to launch an attack on Argentine positions on Mt Longdon, Two Sisters and Mt Harriet on or about 9 June. Logistics continued to be a problem, particularly the stockpiling of artillery ammunition. For an assault Thompson reasoned that each of the task force's 105mm guns required 500 rounds, making a total of 15,000 rounds, the movement of which would require at least 315 Sea King flights. Thompson also believed that 3 Commando Brigade's assault should be supported by 5 Infantry Brigade: the attack of 8 June meant that there would be a delay. On 9 June Major General Moore visited 3 Commando brigade HQ and agreed with Thompson's plan of attack. 3 Commando Brigade was to be reinforced, with 2 Para reverting to Thompson's command, and

Argentine defenders. The performance of the semi-trained 18-year-old conscripts varied greatly. When the fighting started a few curled up in their sleeping bags and adopted the foetal position. But most fired back and many died fighting, if only because during night battles it was well nigh impossible to surrender. (Department of War Studies, Sandhurst)

with the attachment of the Welsh Guards, brought up to strength by two companies of 40 Commando. 3 Commando Brigade was to attack from the west on the night of 10/11 June, while on the following night 5 Infantry Brigade would attack from the more obvious south west.

In Stanley Menendez's attention remained fixed on the south-west route: the activity at Fitzroy and Bluff Cove had served to confirm his conjectures. In Britain the War Cabinet had allowed press speculation about the extent of British casualties to run riot, creating the impression both in Britain and Argentina that they had been very heavy. Menendez came under pressure to attempt an attack towards Fitzroy but firmly resisted. He would remain on the defensive, although he believed the British attack had been seriously delayed.

Menendez had some 9,000 men under his command, of whom about 5,000 were in combat units. The 25th, 6th and 3rd Regiments were stationed along the coast, while the 5th Marine Regiment deployed on Tumbledown, Mt Wilson and Sapper Hill. The 4th Regiment, dug in on Mt Harriet and Two Sisters, covered the approach from Fitzroy and Bluff Cove. Only the 7th Regiment on Mt Longdon and Wireless Ridge was in a position to oppose an attack coming from the west or north-west. By this time air support had virtually vanished. The last Aermacchi flew to the mainland on 30 May and the last two serviceable Chinooks left for the mainland on 9 June. Mainland units had now lost 36 aircraft, and could now only conduct hit-and-run raids. Artillery support, however, remained formidable: 42 105mm and three 155mm guns with approximately 10,000 rounds stockpiled by the guns and more in dumps elsewhere.

The morale and condition of Argentine troops varied enormously. Those based in Stanley, mainly administrative units and air force personnel, enjoyed warm dry accommodation, showers and hot food. Moreover, because they lived amongst the civilian population of Stanley, they were not subjected to shelling and bombing. The troops dug in along the coast had experienced aerial and naval bombardment and were more exposed to the elements, but food was plentiful and they were able occasionally to go into Stanley. But the situation was very different for the troops deployed just seven miles away from Stanley on the hills and mountains to the west and south-west. The first snow had fallen on 1 June and at night temperatures fell to minus 12°C. Some stood up to it better than others. The 5th Marine Regiment (usually based in Tierra del Fuego) coped reasonably well but the 4th Regiment, conscripted in sub-tropical Correntis province, suffered particularly badly. Many conscripts had little idea of fieldcraft and lived in unsanitary, waterlogged trenches – diarrhoea, frostbite, trench foot and exposure were common. The biggest problem was food. Although hundreds of ISO containers in Stanley stood filled with provisions, the Argentine logistic command proved incapable of organising an effective distribution system

Guns of 29 Commando Regiment RA on Mt Kent. Although not as numerous as Argentine artillery, British gunners were trained to a much higher standard. The fire of 29 Commando Regiment was so accurate that the Argentine's believed that the British were assisted by micro-processor-based weapon-location radars. In fact, the only aids the British had were maps, range-finders and compasses. (Department of War Studies, Sandhurst)

for troops just seven miles to the west, who for days at a stretch received nothing more than cold, dehydrated rations. Some administrative troops at a large Argentine depot at Moody Brook moved food forward on their own volition, charging the conscripts exorbitant prices for rations with which they should have been issued. Conscripts responded by forming scavenging parties which pilfered from the depots by night. But movement to and from front-line positions was dangerous – every night British patrols penetrated deeply behind Argentine positions, while British field artillery

and warships kept up harassing fire, which by 10 June had killed 17 Argentines. The morale of the front-line troops was fragile rather than bad. Most had developed a great hatred of administrative units and of their own senior officers, but the shared privations and the long wait in the trenches tended to bond rather than disunite the young conscripts. They now had more rather than less unit cohesion, and by and large were in reasonable physical shape even if uncomfortably dug in. They were also formidably armed.

By the evening of 10 June 3 Commando Brigade was ready to attack. The artillery had stockpiled 11,095 shells and additional fire support was to be provided by automatic 4." guns of four warships, each gun capable of laying down fire equivalent to a battery of six 105mm guns. In all, these ships carried 1,400 rounds. The attack was to develop from north to south – 3 Para at 2000,

42 Commando at 2030 and 45 Commando at 2100. Three Para's commander, Lieutenant Colonel Hew Pike, had been studying the problems of taking his objective, Mt Longdon, for some days. Battalion HQ had built a model of the terrain, and from this it was clear that there was no easy way of taking the feature. From the Paras' positions on the western side of the Murrell River, Mt Longdon appeared to be a peak about 500 yards wide, rising to a crest which towered almost 500 feet over the surrounding moorland. From the eastern side of the peak a narrow ridge some 300 feet high ran back 2,000 yards to a second peak, beyond which lay Wireless Ridge and Port Stanley. Any attempt to attack from the right flank was ruled out, because just to the south over a shallow valley lay Mt Tumbledown, which intelligence had indicated was strongly defended by Argentine Marines. Tumbledown was not due to be attacked until the following night, which meant that 3 Para would be caught in a murderous cross-fire. The alternative, an attack from the north, seemed a better prospect, though the northern side of Mt Longdon was steep, in some places ascending in sheer cliffs 100 feet

British and Argentine dispositions on 11 June 1982

- - - Argentinian unit boundaries
All British guns were 105mm
1 Welsh Guards and 7 Gurkhas
in reserve at Bluff Cove

Mt Vernet

79 Battery
(6 guns)

3 Para

8 Battery
(6 guns)

2 Para
(in reserve)

Mt Kent

45 Cdo

7 Battery
(6 guns)

Mt Longdon

7th

Marine
Heavy Weapons
Platoon

Two Sisters

Mt Tumbledown

Stanley

Airfield

6th

Mt Challenger

Mt Wall

4th
Mt Harriet

Mt William

Sapper Hill

155mm guns,
often moved

Exocet
launcher

(part)
25th

42 Cdo

5th Marine

3rd

29 & 97 Battery
(12 guns)

2 Scots Gds

0   2 miles

0   5 km

N

Before the battle. A Troop Commander of 42 Commando briefs his men near Wall Mountain before the assault on Mt Harriet. Because the battles were to be fought at night in rough terrain it was essential that each man understood his commander's intent, because tight control would not be possible. (Department of War Studies, Sandhurst)

high. Pike decided that he would try a silent approach at night from the north and the west, in the hope that his Paras would reach the lower slopes of Longdon before the Argentines detected them.

From his forward observation post Pike could see that Longdon was a formidable natural obstacle, but he could not see how truly terrible it was. Glaciation, and wind and water erosion had worn into the western peak a network of crevices and gorges which looked like the streets and alleys of a medieval stone village, while the actual peak resembled a bombed-out church. The sides of alleys and re-entrants were riddled with caves, making Longdon a paradise for the defender, a veritable cut-down version of Monte Cassino.

The Argentines had improved many natural features by tearing up a disused tram line, which ran along Stanley Harbour, and using the iron rails to construct top cover – alternate layers of limestone and peat – which had the same protective qualities as compound armour. In addition, Argentine engineers had placed hundreds of anti-personnel mines along all the obvious approach routes. More than 300 Argentines were dug in on Longdon, including a reinforced platoon of the 5th Marines. They had carefully positioned eight 50 calibre heavy machine guns, had a number of 120mm mortars and 105mm recoilless rifles, and could call on indirect fire support from the artillery in and around Stanley.

Shortly after midnight on 11/12 June 3 Para's A and B Companies crossed the startline and began their advance. The night was cold with snow in the wind, but soon the men were sweating. Everyone was carrying extra grenades, rockets and rifle and machine gun ammunition, making the average load about 100 lbs. At first thick clouds obscured the moon, but with 500 yards left to cover the clouds parted and moor and mountain were bathed in pale light. Luck remained with them for a little while longer but then a 4 Platoon section commander, Corporal Brian Milne, stepped on an anti-personnel mine, which blew off his foot. At first only a few Argentine positions opened fire, which suggested that the bulk of the defenders were asleep, and which gave the British a few precious moments to get to the base of the mountain. Here they began to move through the maze of alleys, detecting and destroying some Argentine positions, but being caught in frequent cross-fire as bypassed positions opened up to the rear. Casualties began to mount, officers were hit, and B Company was soon pinned down. With officers now dead and wounded, 4 Platoon Sergeant Ian McKay gathered together four survivors and attacked up the mountain, storming position after position. His companions were soon dead or wounded but McKay pressed on alone over the summit to the northern side of Mt Longdon, where his body was found the following morning, surrounded by dead Argentines. He was to receive a posthumous Victoria Cross.

Meanwhile A Company, attacking on the northern side of the mountain, had run into a heavily defended spur and had gone to ground. Pike withdrew A Company, called in artillery support, and pushed them through

B Company. The Paras began moving again, storming Argentine bunkers one after another, until they controlled the western peak. They now moved eastward, intense fire from Tumbledown to the south forcing them to keep to the northern side of the ridge. A soldier of 3 Para remembered that this phase of the battle

was just like being on a machine gun firing range and everyone was using us as a target. We could see lads going down. I thought, 'Oh my God, this is real.' I'd never seen anything like it before – blokes were being killed, losing limbs and having their intestines blown out.

British artillery fire was now coming down in support, and gradually the Argentines were forced into a grudging retreat from the eastern peak. 3 Para had been fighting for 10 hours, the men were close to exhaustion, but it wasn't over yet. Argentine artillery zeroed in on Longdon, and for the next 36 hours the Paras were subjected to the most sustained artillery

45 Commando yomps across East Falkland. It was more than 50 miles, the Paras carried packs weighing up to 100 lbs, their boots soon began to disintegrate in the peat bogs and they were soaked to the skin by violent squalls. When they reached Teal Inlet a group stood in the sleeting rain and sang a song from Monty Python's *Life of Brian* – 'Always Look on the Bright Side of Life'. (Department of War Studies, Sandhurst)

barrage experienced by the British army since the summer of 1953 in Korea. Taking and holding Longdon, the Argentine's best natural defensive position, cost the Paras 23 dead and more than 50 wounded. Though some conscripts had given up without a fight, most Argentines resisted tenaciously. The majority of the 50 prisoners taken by the Paras were wounded and the British found at least 50 dead.

To the south of Mt Longdon, the Royal Marines of X, Y and Z Companies of 45 Commando had crossed the Murrell River about half an hour after 3 Para had begun its advance, and moved towards Two Sisters. This ridge, with its western and eastern peaks, was potentially a very strong position, along which some 300 Argentines with mortars and heavy machine guns had dug in. The Marine's commander, Lieutenant Colonel Andrew Whitehead, intended that X Company should put in a frontal attack on the westernmost peak to attract the attention of the defenders, while Y and Z Companies came in from the north and hit the Argentines in the right flank. After only a few hundred yards, the heavily laden men of X Company (in addition

to their kit they were carrying 40 Milan missiles, each weighing 30 lbs) found themselves in a maze of bogs and stone cliffs, some 50 to 80 feet high. Men were soon slipping and falling, and one Marine crashed down a 30-foot cliff and was knocked unconscious, though the second-in-command managed to revive him. Meanwhile Y and Z Companies, coming from the north-west over relatively open moorland, had made much better time. Directly to the north, 3 Para's attack on Mt Longdon was now under way, tracer bullets and exploding mortar bombs lighting the sky. Now well behind schedule, X Company moved up the western peak, but about halfway up ran into fire from two machine guns. The Marines lobbed mortar bombs onto the Argentine positions, but after a few rounds the base plates of the mortars dug into the peat, making it impossible to aim the weapons. There was no artillery available,

After the battle. A Royal Marine checks the body of a dead Argentine. Fighting in darkness from holes in the rock and at very close quarters, many Argentines had no option other than to fight to the death. (Department of War Studies, Sandhurst)

so X Company fired its Milan anti-tank missiles at the Argentines, as infantry threaded their way through a maze of boulders to close on their positions.

On the northern slopes of Two Sisters, Y and Z Companies had managed to avoid being hit by an Argentine artillery bombardment, but had been pinned by the fire of 50 calibre heavy machine guns. Argentine mortar bombs now landed just to the rear of Z Company, and the Marines, realising they were bracketed, rose to their feet and shouting the Company war cry 'Zulu! Zulu!' charged up the slope. Y Company joined in the fight, overrunning an enemy machine gun post. Many of the defenders now panicked and some 250 withdrew hurriedly towards Tumbledown. They had suffered 10 dead and 54 wounded. The attacking companies of 45 Commando had overcome a force equivalent to their own strength after suffering only four dead and 10 wounded.

One and a half miles south of Two Sisters lay Mt Harriet, from which the Argentines could dominate the south-western approach to Port Stanley. Visibility was excellent, observers having a bird's-eye view down to the coast, a little more than two miles to the south, while on a clear day they could see as far as Fitzroy and Bluff Cove. The feature, about three-quarters of a mile long, comprised a steep 700-foot horseshoe-shaped peak, with sheer cliffs to the west, and a box canyon to the east. Running several hundred yards further east was a ridge topped by a spine of rocks. About three hundred Argentines had dug in along the ridge, using the stony spine as a battlement. From his forward observation post on Wall Mountain, Lieutenant Colonel Nick Vaux, the commander of 42 Commando, could see that an attack due east would come up against Mt Harriet's most difficult aspect, cliffs which in places were between 50 and 100 feet high. If he went north he ran the risk of a 'blue on blue' with 45 Commando, then moving on Two Sisters. He therefore decided to launch

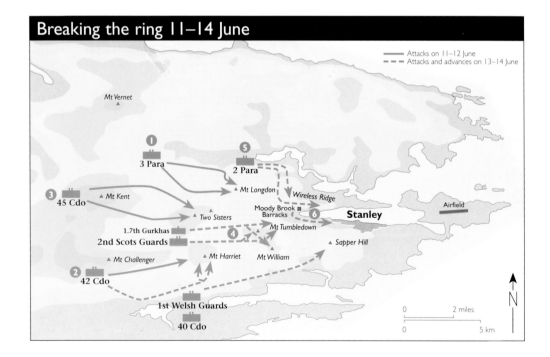

Breaking the ring 11–14 June

Attacks on 11–12 June
Attacks and advances on 13–14 June

1. 3 Para attacks Mt Longdon 11/12 June
2. 45 Commando attacks Two Sisters 11/12 June
3. 42 Commando attacks Mt Harriet 11/12 June
4. 2 Scots Guards attacks Mt Tumbledown 13/14 June
5. 2 Para attacks Wireless Ridge 13/14 June
6. Argentine surrender 2130 (Local Time) 14 June

a diversionary attack due west with
J Company, while he sent 42 Commando's K
and L Companies on an outflanking march
to the south-east. Moving across heavily
mined terrain on previously reconnoitred
routes, K and L Companies skirted the
northern shores of Port Harriet inlet, before
they turned north-west to attack Mt Harriet
from the south-east, the one direction the
Argentines were not expecting.

The Royal Marines had luck on their side.
Vaux had been able to secure artillery
support for his diversionary attack, and this
attracted the attention of the Argentinians.
In addition, the battle for Longdon had
begun seven miles to the north, so that
many of the soldiers had turned around to
watch the explosions and tracer fire. About
700 yards south-east of Mt Harriet, K and
L Companies formed up on a wire fence and
pushed forward. The Argentines were caught
by surprise. The Royal Marines stormed
through the barrier, sending most of the
startled defenders running to the west. The
British pursued them, pushing the
Argentines into the box canyon on the
eastern side of Mt Harriet, from where
there was no escape. The defenders soon
appeared amongst the rocks waving pieces
of white cloth. In all, the British took
250 prisoners, and found a further 10 dead
in the rocks. 42 Commando had suffered
just 11 casualties, of which only one was a
fatality.

At the main command post in Stanley,
the field commander for the Stanley area,
Brigadier General Joffre, had attempted
to launch a counter-attack against
Mt Longdon. At 0300 a company of the
3rd Regiment defending the coast south of
Stanley was ordered to move north to
Moody Brook, and thence by a track to
Mt Longdon. The first part of the move, a
distance of only four miles, took five hours;
dawn was breaking as they prepared to set
off along the track and the move was
cancelled. Joffre had already ordered
Argentine artillery fire down on Longdon,
Two Sisters and Mt Harriet, and his guns
maintained a heavy barrage throughout the

morning. British warships had bombarded
suspected Argentine artillery positions
throughout the night without success,
bringing their fire ever closer to the
western edge of the town; indeed one shell
had landed in the town, killing three
Falkland Islanders. It was against these
warships that the Argentines scored their
solitary success of the night. One of the
bombarding ships, HMS *Glamorgan*,
remained on station later than intended to
support the attack on Two Sisters. In order
to clear Stanley by dawn, her captain took
her just within range of a land-based
Exocet launcher, and she suffered a direct
hit on the stern. Thirteen crewmen were
killed and *Glamorgan* was out of action for
the final hours of the war.

Moore had originally planned to launch
the second phase of the attack, the assaults
on Tumbledown and Wireless Ridge, on the
night of 12/13 June. But British artillery
had expended so much ammunition that
by this stage none of the 30 guns had more
than a few rounds left. It would take a full
day's flying by Sea Kings to restock to just
300 rounds per gun, barely sufficient for
the coming battle. Moreover, many of the
guns needed to be re-sited. They were too
far to the west to give effective support for
the new attacks without using supercharge,
which would shake the lay of the gun and
make fire inaccurate. In addition, in many
places the ground was so soft that after as
few as 30 rounds some guns had sunk up to
the layer's seat, and had simultaneously
moved back as much as 10 yards. The
resiting of the guns was disrupted by
11 Skyhawks sweeping in from the
mainland. Fortunately for the British their
target was not the heavily laden Sea Kings
but 3 Commando Brigade's Headquarters,
upon which they made seven separate
unsuccessful attacks. Brigadier Wilson had
also requested a 24-hour delay to enable
5 Infantry Brigade to conduct a more
detailed reconnaissance of its objective. For
all these reasons Moore decided to
postpone the second phase of the attack
until the night of 13/14 June.

Comrades and companeros

The soldiers who fought in the Falklands, Argentine and British, were literate and many kept diaries and subsequently wrote memoirs. There are several hundred such accounts, in Spanish and in English. Because the vast majority of the veterans are still relatively young (average age for an Argentine is 39, and for a British serviceman is 43) it would be invidious to single out any particular individual as typical. Rather, it is better to present their experiences as a compendium. Much was made of the fact that the Argentine Army was composed of nineteen year old conscripts but most Royal Marines and Paras were only a year or two older. This is not to suggest there was any equivalence in training, fitness or fighting effectiveness – there wasn't. But they were essentially young men fighting a long way from their homes in an alien environment.

Many Argentine troops came from the semi-tropical Correntias province in the far north. The conscripts of the 5th Infantry Regiment had only eight days of military service left when the Junta launched the invasion. When they received orders to fly to the Malvinas soldiers recalled 'a sort of party atmosphere – all your friends were going so you had to go too.' Another remembered that 'only our mothers were really worried and they were crying'. Similar scenes were being played out all over Argentina in the first week of April. The 5th Regiment began flying into Puerto Argentino on 11 April. Very quickly the conscripts realised that despite the hastily imposed Spanish names they were in a foreign country. One was struck by 'how English it all looked. There was nothing Argentine there. I even remember picking up a box of nails which had 'Made in England' on them.' The biggest surprise was the attitude of the people. Many were afraid and virtually all were unfriendly.

The greatest success one Argentine had was 'to establish some communication with one of the locals in my broken English. We communicated like red-skins in the Westerns. "How You?";"You buy";"Is good". And he more or less understood me.'

Except for Tierra del Fuego no part of Argentina is as cold, as windy and as wet as the Falklands. The Argentines were well equipped. They had excellent boots, and warm and generally waterproof parkas bought from the Israeli Defence Force. Those who stayed in Port Stanley – perhaps as many as 5,000 – had a reasonably comfortable time. But from about 1 May the majority had dug into static defence positions. An Argentine private recalled that 'we lived in foxholes and water kept filtering through the peat, so you would find yourself living in the water and ice with no dry clothing. You had to keep as dry as possible and try to eat as much as possible'. At first there was no difficulty but soon British air and naval interdiction began to interfere seriously with attempts to sustain the outlying garrisons, and it was not surprising that they ran short of food. Much more surprising was that many troops in the hills only seven miles from Stanley harbour should have existed for weeks at a time on cold composite rations. Argentine senior officers did hear their men's complaints but dismissed them as the grumbling of nineteen year olds who were used to eating steak three times a day. There was some truth in this but the fact remained that body-weight of many Argentine troops in frontline positions declined precipitously, something which should not have happened given that they were in static defensive positions.

Argentine front-line units spent an average of six weeks living in fox holes, during which a fatal torpor seems to have gripped many. On cold wet mornings they stayed in their sleeping bags inside their pup tents, and paid little or no attention to personal administration. It was up to the officers and NCOs to set and maintain a standard of efficiency, but they were sometimes amongst the worst offenders. The conscripts knew that they should be cleaning their equipment, shaving, washing, patrolling and doing stags throughout the night but they lacked the will to do these things. It was not part of their military culture. Many experienced sustained bombing and shelling, which should have shaken them out of their lassitude, but in many cases seemed to reinforce it.

They would bomb us every night. They would start working their way down, and when they reached the end of our sector they would go back to the front and start all over again. The whole world would seem to be coming on top of you. There was a feeling of impotence, as if you were

The first snow of winter fell on 1 June. Temperatures at night were well below zero. Most soldiers had diarrhoea and had lost between a quarter and a third of their body weight. (Department of War Studies, Sandhurst)

just waiting for death.

And when they did try to counter-attack it was clear their training was woefully deficient.

Then the order arrived for us to go down into the valley. We knew that we would be going into direct combat. Everybody was very agitated and we all talked at the same time. One talked about his sister, another about his college. Someone else talked about football, anything to evade the issue.

The contrast with the British troops could not have been greater. Unlike the Argentines, the Paras and Royal Marines had a six week voyage to get to the Falklands. The *Canberra* is a floating luxury hotel and the *Norland*, though not quite to the same standard, is comfortable. Six weeks on these ship should have destroyed the fighting efficiency of the Paras and Marines but it turned out very differently. At the beginning of the voyage the commanders and their physical training instructors did a computer analysis of every square foot of deck space and instituted a rigorous training programme. Two weeks out of Portsmouth Lieutenant Colonel Hew Pike, commander of 3 Para, recorded in his diary

that the promenade deck of *Canberra*, solid teak two and a half feet thick, was beginning to crack under the impact of the regime. When the Marines and Paras landed at San Carlos they were fitter than they had been in Portsmouth.

At the same time as 3 Para was setting off on its 'tab', 45 Commando was on its 'yomp' across East Falkland. The 'tab-yomp' was a feat of astonishing endurance. The ground underfoot was often peat bog, soft and springy, so that the heavily laden men sometimes sank up to their ankles. Their boots were soon soaked through. The soldier's feet slid around inside their boots, rubbing the skin until it was raw and creating blisters. The weather alternated between brilliant sunshine and sudden drenching rain squalls, with the wind never dropping below about 15 knots. After dark the temperature dropped to below freezing and the rain fell as sleet, driven into the faces of the exhausted men.

Most British soldiers spent about two weeks in positions to the west of Stanley, during which time weather became steadily colder. Logisticians had despatched thousands of arctic tents to the South Atlantic, but had placed most aboard the *Atlantic Conveyor*. With no prospect of tents for some weeks (the first actually arrived on 15 June) the troops improvised. While in transit to the Falklands, each man had been issued with a survival guide to the islands prepared by Major Ewan Southby-Tailyour, whose paper showed how many aspects of the apparently forbidding environment could be turned to advantage. The islands abounded with stones and peat, and soon some of the troops investing Stanley had built themselves a variety of shelters, many of which looked like Celtic roundhouses, and which were suprisingly effective. Lieutenant Tony Martin of the Royal Artillery recorded in his diary for 6 June 'It rained through the night and all this morning. Still, I managed to keep dry in my little house.'

Food, too, proved to be less of a problem than at first feared. The islands have over 600,000 sheep, and all the settlements had potato patches, so that diaries were soon recording dinners of mutton and baked potatoes. The coast was a veritable supermarket, with unpolluted mussels and limpets on virtually every rock, and lobsters and crabs in the shallows. The major deficiency was in fresh vegetables and fruit, though scurvy grass, which grew all over the islands, and is rich in Vitamin C, was eaten by the handful.

Unlike the Argentines, British morale remained high. Whenever they could, they attended to their personal administration, strip washing and shaving. They kept their weapons cleaned and oiled, patrolled aggressively and dominated the ground up to the Argentine positions. The single most important thing in sustaining British morale was the regular arrival of mail. Soldiers received letters not just from families, but from well wishers all over Britain, who wrote to express their appreciation and their pride. It was the first intimation many had that the eyes of the world were literally upon them.

As the time for the final assault drew near the mood of the various regiments was very different. The Scots Guards and Gurkhas were eager to do battle, and the Welsh Guards, the victims of Bluff Cove, were positively thirsting for revenge. It was different with the Royal Marines and Paras, for they had now been in action. The mood, as distinct from the morale, of 2 Para was instructive. On 13 June, as they moved towards the start line for the attack on Wireless Ridge, they were different from the men they had been only three weeks earlier. Then they had been anxious for action, as only professional soldiers who have spent their lives training for this eventuality can be. Since then they had been in a bloody battle and had helped treat the wounded of the Bluff Cove attack. Now there was to be none of the heroics of Darwin–Goose Green. This battle was to be one of the most ruthlessly professional battles fought by the British Army in the twentieth century. The chattering Argentine conscripts moving to meet them on the other side of Wireless Ridge didn't stand a chance.

Preparing for the Third World War

The Falklands conflict involved Britain and Argentina in a struggle for world opinion. Both sides recognised that the support of the United States was vital to their cause, and in this struggle the British Foreign Office, the elite shock troops of the diplomatic world, outgunned Argentine diplomats at every turn. On a visit to the United States in 1981 Galtieri had been fêted by the American military establishment as their special ally in the war against communist expansion in Central America. Argentine advisers were working with US special forces in Nicaragua, and Galtieri, unused to the sometimes overwhelming effusiveness of American hospitality, seems to have believed that this presaged the development of a special relationship with the United States. He forgot, however, that the guerrilla war in Central America was only a small part of America's campaign against the 'Evil Empire'; of much greater importance were simultaneous developments along and just beyond the frontiers of the Soviet empire, and in each of these conflicts the support of Great Britain was vital.

In the three years immediately preceding the Falklands conflict America's position in the Middle East (the area American geopoliticians called South West Asia) had been weakened considerably. On 16 January 1979, following widespread disturbances

In 1982 the Iraqi army was receiving large amounts of equipment from both the USA and USSR. Both super powers preferred the 'progressive and secular' regime of Saddam Hussein to the Islamic revolutionaries of Tehran. (Gamma)

On 1 October 1982 large numbers of semi-trained Iranian Revolutionary Guards launched a major counter-offensive against Iraq. After making some progress, the attack bogged down in sanguinary slaughter. (Gamma)

throughout Iran, the Shah had been driven into exile. Overnight the lynchpin of American policy had been removed. A radical Islamic regime led by Ayatollah Khomeini had taken power, enunciating violently anti-American attitudes. On 4 November 1979 Khomeini's followers stormed the American embassy in Iran, and took nearly 100 embassy staff and Marines hostage. Sixteen days later 500 heavily armed Shi'ite fanatics stormed the Grand Mosque in Mecca within sight of the Kaaba, the holiest place in Islam, and held hostage thousands of pilgrims. Four days later Saudi Arabian troops (supported by western soldiers, it was rumoured) recaptured the Grand Mosque in a ferocious gun battle in which hundreds died. On 21 November a huge mob in Islamabad, believing that the Americans had been involved in the seizure of the Grand Mosque, had stormed the American embassy and were driven off by Pakistani troops only

after considerable bloodshed. And then on 24 December Soviet special forces seized Kabul airport, the prelude to a massive Soviet invasion of Afghanistan.

South West Asia was vital to the American economy, and to the economies of all other industrially developed nations. The United States imported upwards of 40 per cent of its oil requirements from the region, and just five years earlier the Americans had had a terrifying reminder of what life without oil might be like. It was apparent that the result would not just be economic downturn but that the very fabric of civilisation could be torn apart in a matter of weeks. An attempt by US special forces to rescue the hostages in Iran, which ended in a bloody fiasco at a secret base in the Iranian desert on 25 April 1980, served to underline America's impotence in this region. Exactly five months later the Iraqi army invaded Iran; on the night of 25 September the oil refinery at Abadan, the largest in the world, was ablaze. In the previous 18 months oil prices had tripled and seemed set to rise further, thus deepening the recession which was beginning to be felt around the world. It was to Britain, with her wealth of experience in the Middle East, and her residual bases, to which America now turned.

Thus it was that in 1982, while Britain and Argentina battled it out for possession of the Falklands, two major wars were raging in South West Asia. Britain had joined the USA in supplying weapons and training to Afghan rebels. After some hesitation both nations were also supplying Iraq, though Britain also sold weapons to Iran. Of great importance to America were the British Indian Ocean Territories, the largest island of which, Diego Garcia, was rapidly being turned into a huge base from which American and allied forces could be deployed and sustained throughout the Gulf region. A new American command, Central Command, was being set up and was preparing to run a series of deployment exercises codenamed 'Bright Star'.

Of equal concern to Britain and the United States in 1982 was their relationship with the USSR in Europe. Since its formation in October 1980, Solidarity, the new Polish trade union, had shaken communist rule in Poland to its core. In the autumn of 1981 the Soviet leader, Leonid Brezhnev, had issued a grim warning to the Polish Communist Party that the time had come to bring the Solidarity free trade union movement to heel. In December the Polish premier, General Jaruzelski, proclaimed

With the Soviet invasion of Afghanistan into its third year, Afghan guerrillas were receiving large quantities of weapons from the USA and China. An indication of the approaching dissolution of the communist system was the fact that American agents were able to buy substantial numbers of weapons from within the Soviet bloc, before passing them on to their erstwhile allies beyond the Khyber Pass. (Gamma)

martial law, which led to widespread clashes between workers and soldiers in the Silesian coal fields and the Gdansk ship yards, in which at least seven people had been shot. As 1982 dawned more than 14,000 trade union activists had been arrested and imprisoned, the prelude to an outright ban of Solidarity on 8 October.

The United States and Britain had watched the destabilisation of the Soviet empire in Eastern Europe with a mixture of pleasure and apprehension – pleasure because it was an indication of the fragility of the communist system and apprehension because leaders in both countries knew that when empires enter their death throes the result is invariably war. After the failed attempts at conciliation during the Carter presidency, the new Reagan administration was pursuing a policy of confrontation, pushing the Cold War into its last and, in some respects, most dangerous phase. The level of military co-operation between Britain and the USA, always close, had now become intimate. At Fort Monroe in Virginia the US Training and Doctrine Command promulgated a new doctrine for the US Army and Air Force, the doctrine of Airland Battle. Unlike the previous doctrine of Active Defense, which argued that NATO forces should remain on the defensive, Airland Battle argued that allied troops on the inner German border should employ new technology and techniques to strike deep into the heart of Soviet formations, penetrating at least 124 miles (200 km) eastward. Many in Europe had been terrified of what they saw as provocation of the USSR, but British Chiefs of Staff quickly incorporated it into British practice. However, the adoption of the more aggressive American doctrine would only be possible if there were to be a reallocation of the British defence budget. Many senior soldiers could not see the point of having a navy which was capable of supporting world wide commitments when it was obvious that there was massive danger only half an hour's flying time from the United Kingdom. The Royal Navy's role, the soldiers argued, should

be the provision of a forward anti-submarine screen for the United States Navy, and the maintenance of Britain's ultimate deterrent, a squadron of Trident submarines. Hence the suspicion of the alacrity with which the senior officers of the Royal Navy had accepted the challenge of retaking the Falklands.

Britain had also agreed to the United States basing Cruise missiles at various sites in southern England, including the base at Greenham Common outside Newbury. In September 1982 women peace protesters began arriving to set up a peace camp outside the base. At first the local authorities ignored their activities, but as their numbers grew the authorities made two attempts to evict them. On 12 December 1982 the 'Greenham Women' gave a demonstration of how powerful they had become when more than 20,000 protesters surrounded the base and clasped hands. The 'embrace the base' protest attracted enormous media attention, both in Britain and throughout the world. Some of the women tied toys and baby-clothes to the wire, others pinned up photographs of war victims and peace poems. Huge cobwebs of cotton were woven into the fence representing the campaign's symbol of a tiny missile trapped in a web. Herein lay the rebirth of the Campaign for Nuclear Disarmament, whose activities increased dramatically as the Soviet system entered its final stages.

On 6 June 1982, with the attention of the world focused on events in the South Atlantic, six Israeli armoured and mechanised divisions, comprising some 3,000 armoured fighting vehicles and more than 80,000 men, crossed the border into southern Lebanon. Advancing through mountains on roads which were sometimes little better than goat tracks, the Israeli columns were frequently ambushed by the fighters of the Palestine Liberation Organisation (PLO). On 9 June the Israeli Air Force (IAF) attacked and destroyed Syrian anti-aircraft missile batteries in Lebanon's Bekaa Valley, while IAF fighters shot down more than 80 Syrian interceptors for not a single Israeli casualty. This result was only partly the product of superior Israeli training; it was also the product of the new Sidewinder air-to-air missile, the effectiveness of which had just been demonstrated in the fighting in the Falklands.

With undisputed control of the air the Israelis were able to use helicopters to supply their columns and the advance picked up speed. On 11 June, with their tanks and self-propelled guns on the mountains above Beirut, the Israeli army began shelling the city, in an effort to drive out Yassir Arafat and the PLO. The Israelis succeeded, but only after six weeks of bitter fighting, in which scores of Israeli Defence Force (IDF) soldiers and hundreds of Palestinians and Lebanese were killed. On 30 August, 7,000 PLO

fighters began to evacuate the city, firing guns into the air and chanting, as though they had been victorious rather than beaten. As he left by boat for Athens Arafat issued a long farewell message to the Lebanese people, thanking them for the sacrifices they had made in the cause of the Palestinian revolution. 'No matter how much I try,' he said, 'I am still unable to express my gratitude and feelings and admiration towards this country which has embraced our people with love and affection.'

But the departure of the PLO did not bring peace. On 17 September Lebanese Christian militia allied to the IDF began a bloody massacre in the Palestinian refugee camps of

Sabra and Chatila in West Beirut. Men, women and children were ruthlessly shot down, and their bodies thrown in piles in the streets. The IDF claimed that as soon as they knew the massacre was taking place they took steps to stop it, but it was not just the Arab world that remained unconvinced. In the aftermath, US Marines, the French Foreign Legion and Italian forces arrived in Beirut to keep the peace. Here they were joined in December by a small British armoured reconnaissance unit. On 23 October 1983 Hezbollah terrorists drove trucks filled with explosives into the headquarters of the French and American peace-keeping forces and killed themselves

along with 241 US Marines and 58 French paratroopers. Another terrorist drove a truck at the British compound but the military policemen on duty had seen much service in Northern Ireland and shot the driver dead. In a blind rage, America and France lashed out, bombing and shelling suspected Hezbollah positions. All they succeeded in doing was killing more Lebanese civilians, and creating ever more martyrs to be avenged.

During the Falklands conflict Britain still had to contend with terrorism from the IRA. On 20 July, only weeks after the Falklands victory parade, a car bomb exploded on South Carriage Road in Hyde Park, as a detachment of the Blues and Royals trotted by. Two guardsmen were killed and 17 spectators injured. Seven horses were either killed by the blast or had to be destroyed. Two hours later, as the band of the Royal Green Jackets were playing a selection from *Oliver*, another bomb exploded under the bandstand in Regent's Park, killing six soldiers and injuring another 24. One bandsman was hurled nearly 50 yards, his dismembered body impaled on the park railings. Killings in Northern Ireland also continued unabated. The worst incident occurred on 6 December when 16 people, including 11 soldiers, were killed when a bomb ripped through a pub disco in the village of Ballykelly. Interviewed by the BBC's Robert Fox during the fighting at Darwin–Goose Green, a 2 Para NCO said that he was happy to be fighting against soldiers, and not 'the cowards of the IRA'. But the Falklands were only a brief interlude. Most of the Paras who fought in the Falklands were to see service again in Northern Ireland, and some who had survived the mortars and machine guns of Darwin–Goose Green and Longdon were to fall victim to snipers in South Armagh and car bombs in Belfast.

Beirut, 12 June 1982. As the final battles for Stanley were fought, the Israeli army opened fire on PLO positions in Beirut, causing widespread destruction to what had once been the 'Paris of the Arab World'. Televised around the world, the pictures were a propaganda disaster for Israel. (Gamma)

An islander's ordeal: The diary of John Smith

The Falkland Islanders were the first British population to experience enemy occupation of their homeland since the Nazis occupied the Channel Islands in June 1940. John Smith, a manager of the Falkland Islands Company, had first visited the islands in 1957. After several more visits he and his wife Ileen decided to set up a guest house in Stanley. As the crisis unfolded he kept a detailed diary, which recorded the transition from a simple but idyllic existence to the nightmare world of the battlefield. The first intimation of what was to come was when

Falkland Islands children watch a column of Argentine Amtracks grind down a Stanley street. The amount of armour the Argentines felt necessary is testimony to the respect in which they held the Royal Marines. (Gamma)

his oldest sons, Martyn and Jeremy, returned from a trip to Sapper Hill on 1 April, reporting that Royal Marines were taking coils of barbed wire in lorries down towards the airport. That night the Smiths, like everyone else in the Falklands, sat glued to their radios, listening to announcer Mike Smallwood run his Record Requests programme, which he interrupted frequently with messages from the governor. At 2015 Governor Rex Hunt announced that invasion was imminent, and that all members of the Falkland Island Defence Force were to report to the Drill Hall immediately for duty. Smith recorded that his boys looked at each other and said 'This is it'. They struggled into their combat gear and reported to the Drill Hall, only to come back a short time later to pick up rations – tea and sandwiches to last them through the night. It was only then that the reality that his sons were going off to fight alongside the Royal Marines hit Smith. Martyn was just 18. He recorded that the farewell was very swift: 'God Bless and Good Luck said with a depth of sincerity which we hope we will never have to use again.'

At 0540 the governor announced that Argentine landing craft had been sighted. Five minutes later, with dawn breaking, Smith heard the first explosions and firing. He recorded that for the next three hours the firing was more or less continuous. Royal Marines passed by opposite the house, and opened fire up King Street. Smith thought that 'it was just like watching a film. We could not believe that it was happening in front of us on the other side of the road.' The radio provided not just information but first rate drama, because the announcer, Patrick Watts, left the transmitter open as the Argentines stormed the station. 'No, I don't do anything until you take that gun out of my back,' Watts said to the Argentine commandos. 'He deserves a medal' was Smith's pithy comment. He was worried sick about his boys, but all members of the Falkland Islands Defence Force were being held prisoner at their headquarters, and were

being treated correctly. At about 1100 an Argentine captain arrived, congratulated them on a good fight, and they were then escorted back to their homes by Argentine personnel.

The immediate reaction to the invasion was shock. Everything had changed. Argentine amphibious landing vehicles 'were rushing and roaring about all over the place, knocking down fences, breaking up the roads; troops and guns are everywhere. It's like living in a nightmare.' Around midday islanders began venturing out, bits of white cloth tied to sticks, to buy bread at the Upland Goose Hotel. Smith recorded the sense of loss and pride he and others felt as they saw the governor in full regalia, Union Jack flying from his car, drive to the airport. Soon other expatriates were being ordered to leave. With their possessions hurriedly packed into a few suitcases they reminded Smith of refugees. As he walked past Government House on the evening of the first day of the occupation Smith saw the Argentine flag flying from the mast. He 'really felt physically sick and emotionally drained; the cold light of awful reality set in.' On Sunday 4 April the congregation at the evening service in the cathedral sang 'Auld Lang Syne' at the close, which was 'very, very moving'.

Some of the islanders refused to acknowledge the invaders. Mabel Neilson, a formidable old lady, was seen elbowing Argentine soldiers out of the way as they tried to prevent her entering the post office to collect her pension. The weather, too, conspired to discomfort the Argentines. The high wind caused their voluminous ponchos to blow up over their heads, rendering them temporarily blind and completely out of control, 'so much so that a couple of them have accidentally fired their rifles while trying to disentangle themselves'. On 7 April the wind gusted up to 50 knots. With considerable relish Smith reported that 'the huge Argentine flag hoisted on the pole outside the Secretariat flapped itself out of control, snapped the pole and few off in great confusion down Ross Road, chased by anguished soldiers ...'

The Argentines were anxious that the Falklanders should wish to become part of Argentina, and put into effect a crude 'hearts and minds' programme. An Anglo-Argentine delegation arrived, proposing that a new town be built for the islanders some distance from Stanley, which would have a sports complex, swimming pool and many other modern amenities. The islanders remained unconvinced. A public meeting at which the Argentines outlined the plan turned into a 'fiery affair'. Smith's entries are suffused with the contempt he felt for these people. 'They [the Anglo-Argentines] want to have the best of both sides. Although most frightfully British, they are completely in the grip of the

Delighted Argentines display their flag in Stanley. For a short time they joined the select band of warriors who had defeated the British in battle. Islanders recorded that they felt physical shock when they saw the Argentine flags, and got a savage satisfaction when high winds blew away the largest of them. (Rex Features)

English-language Argentine news programmes, but were quickly seduced by American and British films.

At first the occupation was irritating rather than oppressive, but as the task force came closer, conditions became worse. Scores of people began leaving Stanley for stations on the 'camp', the islanders term for the country, until by the middle of May the population had been reduced to fewer than 600. Stanley filled with troops (there were eventually more than 3,000 in the town) who were digging bunkers and constructing fortifications with increasing urgency. Smith had at first tried to identify Argentine shipping and aircraft with his binoculars, and had even taken photographs, but he decided that it was now too dangerous. Argentine special police arrived, who began to arrest anyone they deemed to be behaving suspiciously. On one occasion an attempt was made to arrest Smith himself, and it was only his personal appeal to a senior Argentine officer who had been a friend which prevented him being sent to a detention centre. The restrictions imposed by the military government became steadily worse – identification papers, curfews, compulsory blackouts, confiscation of radios, requisitioning of civilian vehicles and spot checks.

On 25 April Smith tuned in to the BBC World Service (most islanders kept clandestine radios) and learned that South Georgia had been retaken. 'The weather might be lousy but the news is superb' he wrote. It was now clear that the British would come, and that there would probably be a battle for Stanley. Smith and his friends formed a volunteer fire brigade (they were issued with armbands on which was painted 'Bombero-Fireman') and they began hacking a bunker out of a stone run in Smith's

Argentines. They don't appear to have any real loyalty; only a noxious mixture of greed and snobbery, probably more dangerous than the Argentines themselves.' More successful was the Argentine's introduction of television to Stanley, with an offer of a colour television set for a deposit of only £20. The islanders were deeply suspicious of garden. By late April sporadic shooting could be heard at night, possibly clashes between the garrison and British special forces, but more likely nervous Argentine conscripts firing away at shadows. At 0447 on 1 May the war really arrived. Smith recalled 'we were literally thrown out of our beds by the most fearful explosions. The house seemed to lift off its foundations.' There were now 11 people living in the house - John Smith, his wife and two sons, and seven neighbours, who had banded together for mutual support and protection. All now rushed for the bunker and threw themelves through the entrance. It was now to be their home for many nights. At dawn Smith left his shelter to make a cup of tea, and witnessed 'a bunch of Harriers streaking in through the harbour entrance almost at sea level at a truly incredible speed. The water and earth boiled with their cannon-fire; then they let go their bombs on the airfield ... The most fantastic sight I have ever seen.'

Harrier and Vulcan raids and shelling from warships soon became the backdrop of life. By 7 May many shelves in the West store were becoming noticeably emptier, but there was no sign of panic buying or hoarding. Smith observed that 'there is an air of much greater companionship among everyone; we all seem to have a lot more trust and a lot more faith in one another –war is a great leveller.' By 15 May Smith could report that 'everyone in town is rather blasé about bombs now; we all turn out to watch.' The feeling didn't last long. A short time later a naval shell smashed into a house, killing two women outright, and seriously wounding another, who died later.

On 21 May, the morning of the landings, Smith reflected upon 'how odd it seemed to hear San Carlos mentioned on the world news'. By the end of the month Stanley was beginning to look like a town that had been through a war. Heavy Argentine vehicles had cracked the road surfaces, and a series of hard frosts had then finished the job. The

autumn rains had converted the holes to quagmires, and then the boots of thousands of marching Argentines had smeared the mud around the town. Increasing numbers of islanders spent the nights with friends in bunkers, only to discover in the morning that Argentine soldiers had broken into their homes, smashing furniture, lighting fires and leaving the walls smeared with excrement. By the end of the month the supply of both water and electricity had become intermittent, and petrol had virtually disappeared. Islanders now filled up butts from downpipes, read by candlelight and travelled by bicycles. As the British got closer Smith noticed more and more Argentines visiting the church.

Some come to pray for a few minutes, some just to sit and shake. One sat in front of us shaking and trembling in a combination of exhaustion, fear and cold. Another cried uncontrollably. Most are very young.

By the end of the first week in June Argentine security police were visiting homes at night, checking that British special forces had not infiltrated into the civilian population. Smith found the knock on the door after dark 'all very sinister, rather like the sort of things you read about in books but never expect to happen to you.' On 12 June Smith recorded that the 'intensity of the shelling is such that the whole town seems to be shaking'. The bombardment never let up and 'it's getting a bit trying on the nerves'. The following day was Sunday and Smith attended church. On his walk back through the broken, filthy streets, guns roaring in the hills a few miles distant, he found it 'difficult to grasp that all this was happening in our once serene and tranquil Stanley. It was like having a nightmare – sitting on the outside of a situation looking in, paralysed, unable to do anything whatsoever to stop this awful holocaust which hourly is increasing in its violence, so that soon it must explode in a great fury all around us.'

The mind of Menendez

In the evening of 14 June three battalions moved to resume the attack. The main effort this time was to be by 5 Infantry Brigade, with 2nd Scots Guards assaulting Tumbledown and 1/7th Gurkhas following through to Mt William, which was a spur stretching south-east of Tumbledown. Meanwhile 2 Para, which had acted as 3 Commando Brigade's reserve on 10/11 June, was to attack Wireless Ridge. Tumbledown Mountain was a rocky ridge beginning three miles west of Stanley and extending one and a half miles due west. The northern edge of the ridge ended in steep cliffs, making any assault from this direction difficult. The approach from the south-west was much easier. Tumbledown–Mt William were the keys to the defence of Stanley from any attack from the west or south-west. Consequently it was here that Joffre had dug in his best unit, the 5th Marines, who could

When they entered Stanley the Marines and Paras were shocked by the condition of the town. Very little damage was the result of the British bombardment. Argentine vehicles had torn up the roads, turning them into quagmires, and in the last stages of the occupation undisciplined Argentine soldiers had comprehensively trashed many houses. (Department of War Studies, Sandhurst)

An Argentine 105mm gun knocked out by British counter-battery fire. Though they had more artillery and much more ammunition, Argentine gunners invariably came off second best in artillery duels. They managed to keep their casualties relatively low by positioning most of their ordnance in the streets of Stanley. (Department of War Studies, Sandhurst)

call on very considerable artillery assets positioned only some five miles away. In addition, the western and south-western approaches had been heavily mined.

The Scots Guards commander, Lieutenant Colonel Mike Scott, sent a platoon of guards and four light tanks in a diversionary attack along the Fitzroy–Stanley track. It had the desired effect. One tank was destroyed by a mine and the platoon attracted heavy machine gun, mortar and artillery fire; it suffered two dead and nine wounded. The 5th Marines had only one man killed and for a time believed they had stopped the main British assault.

Meanwhile G Company Scots Guards made a silent approach to the western end of the ridge and without being detected occupied almost one-third of Tumbledown. Major John Kiszley's Left Flank Company then took over and for 30 minutes continued the advance unopposed. Now about halfway along the ridge, they ran into the main Argentine position. Fire was intense and Left Flank Company went to ground, unable to move. Kiszley attempted to call down artillery, but in the dark and confusion could not find his Forward Observation Officer. Back at battalion HQ the artillery liaison officer tried to direct a bombardment but he was too far back to do this effectively and one of the guns was firing rogue, as much a danger to the Scots Guards as it was to the 5th Marines. The stalemate went on for three hours. Lying on the mountainside next to his signaller Kiszley felt the intense cold give way to numbness and realised that hypothermia was approaching. Overcoming their inhibitions, Kiszley and his signaller snuggled together, to warm each other up. As an Argentine shell landed nearby, Kiszley recalled that his signaller, an irrepressible Cockney, expressed some misgivings. 'Ere sir' he said, 'Wot are people gonna fink if we get killed and they find our bodies like this!' Realising that more and more of his men would succumb to the cold, Kiszley sent his 13 Platoon to collect up as many rocket launchers and machine guns as they could find, and work their way along the left flank.

13 Platoon lined up at least 10 66mm anti-tank rocket launchers, loosed a volley, and with Kiszley in the lead 14 and 15 Platoons attacked. Tumbledown was a series of false crests – as they reached one another appeared. In this manner they covered another 800 yards. Positions were overrun, prisoners were taken, and Kiszley had to detach more and more men to escort them to the rear. When he finally reached his objective, a rocky ledge which was the highest part of the ridge, Kiszley had just six men with him. Having spent the last two weeks in a wilderness of stone runs and peat bogs, the men looked down into Stanley, the street lights demarcating the pattern of the town. They stood stock still and stared. At that moment a burst of machine gun fire wounded three of the men. Before 5th Marines had realised the weakness of the British position, Major Simon Price's Right Flank Company moved up to take over the attack. His technique was basically the same as Kiszley's – a platoon left flanking to provide fire support, while his other two platoons pushed on destroying sangers with rocket launchers and grenades. More than 11 hours after crossing the start line the Scots Guards had pushed the 5th Marines off Tumbledown. The Guards had lost seven killed and 40 wounded, the 5th Marines some 30 killed and 14, mainly wounded, captured.

While the Scots Guards' battle raged, 2 Para, now commanded by Lieutenant Colonel David Chaundler, was moving on Wireless Ridge, which extended east–west about a mile to the north of Tumbledown. The Argentines here were the 7th Regiment, some of whom were survivors of the battle for Mt Longdon. In all, about 500 were dug in. The British plan involved a subsidiary attack by D and G Squadrons SAS in Royal Marine rigid raiders across Hearndon Water, an inlet to the north of Stanley Harbour. Illuminated by a searchlight on an Argentine hospital ship, the SAS came under intense fire both from the eastern slopes of Wireless Ridge and from massed anti-aircraft batteries north of Stanley acting in the direct fire role.

In these circumstances it was surprising that the SAS were able to withdraw with only three wounded. Like the Scots Guards' diversion, this attack convinced some Argentines that they had beaten off a long anticipated direct assault on Stanley.

The main attack on Wireless Ridge was supported by the heaviest concentration of firepower the British had massed thus far. During the course of the battle British field artillery pumped 6,000 105mm shells onto Wireless Ridge, while two frigates lobbed about 600 4.5in shell on to the eastern slopes. The paratroopers advanced with the support of two Scorpions and two Scimitars, which kept up a constant stream of 76 and 30mm cannon fire and 7.62mm machine gun fire, until all four tanks had to withdraw to restock. All the mortars of 3 Para were attached to those of 2 Para and kept up a near continuous arc of bombs, while a machine gun platoon firing in support expended more than 40,000 rounds and came close to burning out three General Purpose Machine Guns. As one paratrooper commented, it was like 'a Warminster firepower demonstration'. Under the weight of this fire Argentine morale cracked; 2 Para met little resistance until D Company reached the highest part of the ridge. Even here the battle was soon over. The paratroopers lost 14 men, three of whom were killed. Nearly 100 Argentine dead were found in positions on the ridge and another 37, mainly wounded, were taken prisoner. The remainder of the Argentines were now fleeing in broad daylight down the track to Stanley.

Menendez and Joffre had been heartened during the night by reports that a British amphibious landing and an armoured attack along the Fitzroy–Stanley track had been repulsed. But around dawn the true situation was very clear. The remnants of 7th Regiment were fleeing back from Wireless Ridge while the last marines had withdrawn from Tumbledown. Argentine artillery responded vigorously and Joffre sent 3rd Regiment west of Stanley to counter-attack Wireless Ridge. It was a half-hearted attack and soon 3rd Regiment was hurrying back to Stanley.

To the British it suddenly became clear that the Argentine front had collapsed; they kept up the pressure. While 2 Para followed the fleeing mass down off Wireless Ridge, the Gurkhas advanced up Mt William and were disappointed to find that, here too, the Argentines had withdrawn. In a daring move, 45 Commando were lifted by helicopter on to Sapper Hill, the last position before Stanley on which defence was possible, and occupied it without resistance. Four Scout helicopters swept over Moody Brook – the first time helicopters had been used directly over the battlefield since the day of the landings – and attacked Argentine batteries with SS-11 missiles. Meanwhile an SAS team, infiltrated on to Seal Point near Stanley Harbour, directed artillery fire on to the retreating Argentines and on to likely forming-up places. To this intense physical pressure, the British now added psychological pressure. Nine days earlier Captain Rod Bell, a Spanish-speaking officer, had begun radio transmissions and had established direct contact with Argentine officers in Stanley. From 0900 Bell was on the radio link offering the Argentines a ceasefire on humanitarian grounds and negotiations to discuss honourable terms.

Menendez had at first toyed with the idea of pulling out of Stanley and holding the airfield. He still had three battalions that had not been in combat and ample food and munitions for a very long siege. Indeed, although he did not know it, he still had more artillery than the British, and his logistic situation was very much better than that of his enemy. At about 1100 he managed to get a radio link to Galtieri to discuss the situation. Galtieri reasoned that British logistics must be close to breaking and that Menendez should counter-attack with all the forces at his disposal. In order to spur Menendez the president reminded him of the Argentine military code which stipulated that a commander should fight until he had lost 50 per cent of his men and expended 75 per cent of his ammunition, and then added, 'the responsibility today is with you.' It was at this point that Menendez's morale finally broke. According to the transcript of the conversation, he replied, 'I cannot ask more of my troops, after what they have been through ... We have not been able to hold on to the heights ... We have no room, we have no means, we have no support ...' Believing himself deserted by his government and psychologically isolated, Menendez turned almost gratefully to the Spanish-speaking British officer on another radio link and agreed to meet Moore's emissaries that afternoon. After preliminary negotiations the surrender was signed at 2115.

It was a very much closer run thing than Menendez realised. British guns were quite literally down to their last few rounds, and many soldiers had received no rations for 72 hours. Only the day before Woodward had warned Moore that his task force was on its last legs. The admiral had confided to his diary, 'We are now on the cliff edge of our capability ... Frankly, if the Argies could only breathe on us, we would fall over! Perhaps they're the same way: can only trust so, otherwise we're in for a carve up.' On 14 June 1982 the British were digging deep into their resources but were determined to finish it; the Argentines possessed the logistic apparatus to carry on fighting for several more weeks, but their desire to win had evaporated.

Interviewed by the BBC on the following day Moore reflected upon the fact that he at last understood the stress Clausewitz had placed on the 'moral' factors in war. His men had literally killed the Argentine will to fight.

Royal Marines raise the Union Jack outside Government House. The Falklands War was unusual for the late twentieth century, in that it had a definite beginning and a definite end, indicated by the removal of the union flag on 2 April and its restoration on 15 June. (Rex Features)

Thatcher's triumph: It was a famous victory

War had come because Argentina had misinterpreted the position and hence the actions of the British government in the first three months of 1982. Argentina simply could not believe that the British would respond to Operation Rosario by dispatching a powerful task force, but nor could most international observers. There was a failure at two levels; the Junta did not understand the dynamics of British party politics and it did not appreciate the strength of a tradition which, when similar situations had arisen in the past, had impelled Britain to go to war. The Junta always seemed to be surprised by Britain's responses, having failed to understand that Operation Rosario had imposed on the Thatcher government a choice between victory or political death.

For the British the Falklands campaign was an extremely desperate operation, far more desperate than was generally understood at the time. Woodward, Moore, Thompson, Clapp and the other commanders knew they had to win but they were not at all sure how they would win. The task force was to operate on an insecure 8,000-mile supply line, the ships could only maintain station for about six weeks, the strike aircraft of the Argentine Air Force outnumbered British fighters by about four to one, and the South Atlantic winter was fast approaching. Fortunately the Argentines made a number of mistakes. They completely failed to understand the precarious nature of British logistics and insisted on attacking the warships. Had they sunk *Atlantic Causeway* and *Elk* as well as *Atlantic Conveyor* it is difficult to see how the British could have finished the campaign before Woodward's task force fell to pieces. Similarly, had more Argentine bombs detonated, British losses may have become unsustainable. Argentine pilots were amongst the best in the world,

and many Argentine infantry battalions, well supplied with weapons and ammunition in excellent defensive positions, fought with courage and determination. By the standards of many other conscript armies the Argentines were very good; it was just that the British were very much better, not in weaponry or logistics, but in terms of training, confidence and professional pride. The British inflicted nearly 14,000 casualties on the Argentines, of whom some 2,000 were killed or wounded. But it was not a cheap victory. More than 1,000 British became casualties, approximately 4 per cent of the task force, of whom 255 were killed.

The consequences for both belligerents were dramatic and long lasting. When the news that Menendez had surrendered broke in Argentina on 15 June huge crowds gathered in the Plaza de Mayo in Buenos Aires, screaming 'Cowards' and 'Sons of Bitches' at the soldiers who tried to disperse them. The authority of the army had evaporated overnight. No longer afraid, a mob attempted to storm the presidential palace. On 17 June Galtieri was ousted as president after 12 out of 14 senior generals voted at a meeting in Buenos Aires to use only diplomacy to regain the Malvinas. Thereafter the structure of military rule unravelled rapidly; on 30 October 1983 the Radical Party led by Raoul Alfonsin gained an absolute majority in democratic elections. On 22 April 1985 Galtieri and nine colleagues were placed on trial for crimes committed during the dictatorship, and sentenced to various terms of imprisonment.

As the ships of the task force returned to Britain during the summer of 1982, the servicemen were astonished by the reception they received. Huge crowds gathered at Portsmouth to cheer the ships in, hundreds of thousands cheered a victory parade in

The people of Argentina were also direct beneficiaries of the British victory. Within months
the military regime had been swept away and democracy had been reintroduced. (Gamma)

Troops returning on *Canberra* were astounded by the size of the crowds that were waiting for them, and the enthusiasm they displayed. The men of the task force had been completely unaware that the entire world had been following the campaign hour by hour, and that to British people they were now heroes. (Gamma)

London, and for months afterwards veterans of the South Atlantic Campaign found that they did not have to buy a drink in a pub. The public rejoicing reflected more than exultant jingoism. Since 1945 a sense of inexorable decline had been growing in Britain, and since the mid-1970s it had been accelerating. In the summer of 1981 the worst riots in more than a century and a half

had torn through more than 40 British cities, and in early 1982 a recession began to bite hard with industries collapsing and unemployment passing the three million mark for the first time since the early 1930s. The stunning victory in the Falklands gave many in Britain a renewed sense of pride in their country and a feeling that the decline might not be terminal – that perhaps the bottom had been reached and that Britain would now begin to fight her way back to her former standing.

That was certainly the message propounded by Mrs Thatcher, the greatest beneficiary of the Falklands War. She had

For the first time since June 1946 British troops marched through London to celebrate a victory. When the task force had sailed national morale was at an all time low. The armed forces had at last given British people something of which they could be proud. (Rex Features)

risked everything on an outright British victory, and now reaped the rewards. The Conservatives carefully avoided mentioning the Falklands in the 1983 general election, but the imagery they employed in the campaign, dark blue aircraft carrier shapes on light blue backgrounds, stirred memories that were still fresh. In a move of astonishing ineptitude some Labour MPs attacked various aspects of the Prime Minister's handling of the war, and suffered the consequences – a massively increased Conservative majority. Now firmly established in the premiership, Mrs Thatcher disposed of likely rivals, starting with Francis Pym, and then steadily working her way through the so-called 'wets'. The Falklands

ushered in another 15 years of Conservative rule, an enormous success which in the end seriously damaged the party's cohesion.

The British armed forces also benefited. The Nott Defence Review was quietly shelved, Nott himself became a political casualty, and the Royal Navy got and kept three carriers. But the impact was not merely in terms of equipment. The relationship between Britain's armed forces and the British public had always been problematic – the people were warlike but unmilitary. Despite the success of the SAS in occasional highly publicised operations, the general view of the British armed forces held by the British public before the spring of 1982 was that they were brave but incompetent. The disaster of Suez, and the disasters in the first three years of the Second World War and for much of the First World War, had informed the memories of three generations. Now new armed forces seemed to have emerged, efficient, cunning, intelligent, competent and courageous. Public approval of the armed forces rose rapidly, and remained high for the rest of the century, as the middle and junior commanders of the campaign began to achieve high rank.

Perhaps the greatest compliments paid to the British armed forces came from Britain's greatest adversary and her closest ally. Nowhere did the news of Darwin–Goose Green have a greater impact than in the Soviet Union. Soviet analysts studied the battle intensively, and decided on this basis that they had considerably underestimated the fighting power of the British Army of the Rhine. Beginning in the autumn of 1982 Warsaw Pact forces facing the British in northern Germany began to receive substantial reinforcements. Equally impressed, the United States began moderating its post-Vietnam objections to military interventions, and in 1983 sent Marines to the Lebanon and launched an invasion of Grenada, lest Cuba and the USSR build bases on the tiny island state. Both operations went wrong. In Beirut the Marines suffered 241 dead in a terrorist attack, while in Grenada landings of special forces and paratroopers degenerated into an embarrassing shambles, so much so that the ground force commander, General Norman

Schwarzkopf, issued an open apology to the units involved. He was to oversee the rebirth of American military prowess, but not for another seven years.

But the people on whom the war had the greatest impact were the Falkland islanders. Their way of life, not unlike that of nineteenth-century Highland crofters, was gone forever. In the summer of 1982 there were about 25,000 people on the islands, ten times the number who had ever lived on the Falklands before. At the end of the fighting Britain had to maintain a substantial garrison, which entailed regular flights from Brize Norton, and a much more regular shipping service. Expanded radio services and television soon followed, along with massively increased visits by tourists, surveying the battlefields, watching the wild life, walking across the moors, and fishing. Tracks were soon metalled, and family cars were seen alongside the ubiquitous land rover. The greatest change was the beginning of systematic large scale exploration for oil, with rumours of fields which would make those of the North Sea look like puddles. Should this come to pass the natives of the Falklands will become the richest people on Earth, capable perhaps of buying the Royal Navy – or Argentina.

Select bibliography

Brown, D., 'The Royal Navy and the Falklands War', London, 1987.

Burden, R.A., M.I. Draper, D.A. Rough, C.R. Smith and D. Wilton 'Falklands: the Air War' ,London, 1986.

Freedman, L., and Virginia Gamba-Stonehouse 'Signals of War: The Falklands Conflict of 1982', London, 1990.

McManners, Hugh, Falklands Commando, London,

Middlebrook, M., 'Operation Corporate: The story of the Falklands War, 1982',London, 1985.

– 'The Fight for the Malvinas: The Argentine Forces in the Falklands War', London, 1989.

Smith, J., 'Seventy Four Days: An Islander's Diary of the Falklands Occupation', London, 1984.

Thompson, J., 'No Picnic. 3 Commando Brigade in the South Atlantic 1982', London, 1985.

West, N., 'The Secret War For The Falklands', London, 1997.

Woodward, Sir John, 'One Hundred Days: The memoirs of the Falklands Battle Group Commander', London, 1992.

Index

Other titles in the Essential Histories series

The Crusades
ISBN 1 84176 179 6

The Crimean War
ISBN 1 84176 186 9

The Seven Years' War
ISBN 1 84176 191 5

The Napoleonic Wars (1) The rise of the Emperor 1805–1807
ISBN 1 84176 205 9

The Napoleonic Wars (2) The empires fight back 1808–1812
ISBN 1 84176 298 9

The French Revolutionary Wars
ISBN 1 84176 283 0

Campaigns of the Norman Conquest
ISBN 1 84176 228 8

The American Civil War (1) The war in the East 1861–May 1863
ISBN 1 84176 239 3

The American Civil War (2) The war in the West 1861–July 1863
ISBN 1 84176 240 7

The American Civil War (3) The war in the East 1863–1865
ISBN 1 84176 241 5

The American Civil War (4) The war in the West 1863–1865
ISBN 1 84176 242 3

The Korean War
ISBN 1 84176 282 2

The First World War (1) The Eastern Front 1914–1918
ISBN 1 84176 342 X
January 2002

The First World War (2) The Western Front 1914–1916
ISBN 1 84176 347 0
January 2002

The Punic Wars 264–146 BC
ISBN 1 84176 355 1
February 2002

The Falklands War 1982
ISBN 1 84176 422 1
February 2002

The Napoleonic Wars (3) The Peninsular War 1807–1814
ISBN 1 84176 370 5
March 2002

The Second World War (1) The Pacific
ISBN 1 84176 229 6
March 2002

The Iran-Iraq War 1980–1988
ISBN 1 84176 371 3
April 2002

The French Religious Wars 1562–1598
ISBN 1 84176 395 0
June 2002

The First World War (3) The Western Front 1916–1918
ISBN 1 84176 348 9
June 2002

The First World War (4) The Mediterranean Front 1914–1923
ISBN 1 84176 373 X
July 2002

The Second World War (2) The Eastern Front 1941–1945
ISBN 1 84176 391 8
July 2002

The Mexican War 1846–1848
ISBN 1 84176 472 8
July 2002

The Wars of Alexander the Great
ISBN 1 84176 473 6
July 2002

Praise for Essential Histories

'clear and concise' *History Today*

'an excellent series' *Military Illustrated*

'Osprey must be congratulated on Essential Histories' *Soldier*

'very useful, factual and educational' *Reference Reviews*

'valuable as an introduction for students or younger readers ... older readers will also find something 'essential' to their understanding' *Star Banner*

'accessible and well illustrated...' *Daily Express*

'... clearly written ...' *Oxford Times*

'they make the perfect starting point for readers of any age' *Daily Mail*

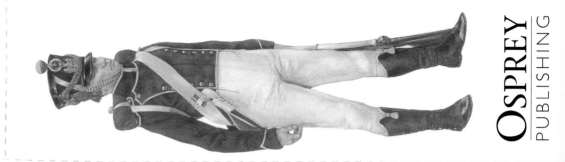

OSPREY PUBLISHING

FIND OUT MORE ABOUT OSPREY

❏ Please send me a FREE trial issue of Osprey Military Journal

❏ Please send me the latest listing of Osprey's publications

❏ I would like to subscribe to Osprey's e-mail newsletter

Title/rank _____

Name _____

Address _____

_____

_____

_____

Postcode/zip _____

State/country _____

E-mail _____

Which book did this card come from?

_____

❏ I am interested in military history

My preferred period of military history is _____

❏ I am interested in military aviation

My preferred period of military aviation is _____

I am interested in (please tick all that apply)

❏ general history   ❏ militaria   ❏ model making

❏ wargaming   ❏ re-enactment

Please send to:

USA & Canada:
Osprey Direct USA, c/o Motorbooks International,
PO Box 1, 729 Prospect Avenue, Osceola, WI 54020, USA

UK, Europe and rest of world:
Osprey Direct UK, PO Box 140, Wellingborough,
Northants, NN8 2FA, United Kingdom

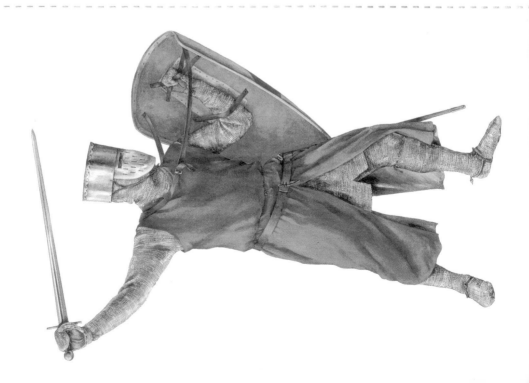

OSPREY
PUBLISHING

www.ospreypublishing.com

call our telephone hotline
for a free information pack

USA & Canada: 1-800-458-0454
UK, Europe and rest of world call:
+44 (0) 1933 443 863

Young Guardsman
Figure taken from *Warrior 22:
Imperial Guardsman 1799–1815*
Published by Osprey
Illustrated by Richard Hook

Knight, c.1190
Figure taken from *Warrior 1: Norman Knight 950 – 1204AD*
Published by Osprey
Illustrated by Christa Hook

POSTCARD